Friendship QUILTS
BY HAND AND MACHINE

Friendship QUILTS
BY HAND AND MACHINE

How to Organize, Make, Assemble and Display Friendship Quilts ∽

CAROLYN VOSBURG HALL

CHILTON BOOK COMPANY RADNOR, PENNSYLVANIA

Designed by William E. Lickfield
Manufactured in the United States of America

Library of Congress Cataloging in Publication Data
Hall, Carolyn Vosburg, 1927–
  Friendship quilts by hand and machine.
  (Creative machine arts series)
  Bibliography: p. 200
  Includes index.
  1. Friendship quilts. I. Title. II. Series.
TT835.H325 1987   746.9'7   86-47932
ISBN 0-8019-7784-3 (pbk.)

Other books in the Creative Machine Arts Series, available from Chilton:

The Complete Book of Machine Embroidery, by Robbie and Tony Fanning
Creative Nurseries Illustrated, by Debra Terry and Juli Plooster
Creative Serging Illustrated, by Pati Palmer, Gail Brown and Sue Green
The Expectant Mother's Wardrobe Planner, by Rebecca Dumlao
The Fabric Lover's Scrapbook, by Margaret Dittman
Know Your Bernina, by Jackie Dodson
Pizzazz for Pennies, by Barb Forman

1 2 3 4 5 6 7 8 9 0   7 6 5 4 3 2 1 0 9 8

To the friends who made the
550 quilt blocks in this book;
Leslie, Rosemary, Helen, and Lois
for "mothering" quilts;
Bob Vigiletti for his
outstanding photographs;
my daughter, Claudia Hall Stroud,
for design assistance;
and my husband, Cap Hall,
for every kind of assistance.

Contents

Chapter 4
Ways to Include Friends
Kim's Valentine Quilt

Chapter 5
Choosing Colors
Lori's Wedding Quilt

Chapter 6
Fabrics Plain and Fancy
Louise's Antique Crazy Quilt

Chapter 7
Tools for Patchwork
Hattie's Birthday Quilt

Chapter 8
Hand and Machine Appliqué
The Artists' Quilt

Chapter 9
Embroidery by Hand
and Machine
Amy's Wedding Quilt

Chapter 10
Cross-Stitch,
Crayon Transfer,
Stenciling,
Novelty Techniques
A Quilt Quintet

Foreword

The approaching birth of a treasured friend's baby, the wedding of two special people, a 50th anniversary to celebrate—all these occasions and more prompt us fabric-lovers to commemorate it: as author Carolyn Hall says, it's like Mickey Rooney and Judy Garland shouting, "Hey kids! Let's rent a barn and make a friendship quilt!"

But when it comes time to organize the initial impulse, woe! How big should the quilt be? Who should be included? What colors? Should we buy the fabric or should we let the participants use their own? What if they can't stitch?

The beauty of this book is that Carolyn has anticipated all of your questions. She methodically shows you how to design, organize, make, assemble, and display any type of friendship quilt you feel inspired to tackle. Each chapter covers one aspect of planning, with a representative quilt shown. By studying these quilts and how they were made, you will learn what to include and what to avoid in your own quilts.

I especially like three aspects of this book:

1. While Carolyn covers appliqué blocks, embroidered blocks, and pieced blocks, she also discusses stumbling blocks and mental blocks. Some of your friends will freeze up over their blocks; Carolyn shows how to help them. And if you're having qualms, too, her design checklist in Chapter 3 is a godsend.

2. Hand quilting, though beautiful, takes forever. I appreciate Carolyn's thorough information on machine embroidery, machine appliqué, and machine quilting. It makes it possible to deliver friendship quilts at the baby shower, instead of when the kid enters nursery school.

3. You don't have to be a quilter to participate. Carolyn shows how to include men, children, co-workers, and other non-fabric people (see especially Chapter 10).

All of this puts the emphasis where it belongs: not on perfect technique, but on the heartfelt expression of friendship.

Robbie Fanning

Creative Machine Arts Series Editor
and co-author,
The Complete Book of Machine Embroidery

Preface

When my daughter Claudia announced her engagement, my friend Leslie Masters and I decided to maker her a friendship quilt with squares contributed by all her friends and relatives. Inspiration came from a lovely 1892 crazy quilt my mother had given me not long before. Scattered about on the quilt face were names carefully embroidered by a group of ladies during the 1890s on colorful, rich fabrics typical of that era.

Now, nearly 100 years later, my daughter was getting married and I felt the same urge to share in this rite of passage. To Leslie's and my surprise, we found all those we asked to contribute squares as eager as we were. At the time, we didn't realize that a surge of friendship-quilt-making was once again abroad in the land. Neither Leslie nor I had made a friendship quilt before, but we had been involved with a group quilt for our town organized by Rosemary Squires, an enormous task full of research on local history. We planned nothing so elaborate for Claudia, just a potpourri of quilt blocks from friends.

Also, we had each made many quilts and other fiber artworks before, although we don't consider ourselves expert "quilters." Leslie paints sensuous color field paintings, and I've been a fiber artist for years, specializing in soft sculptures. In 1978, the editor of my first three books, Rachel Martens, convinced me I could make a quilt in one day. That was one wild day—six strenuous hours, not counting shopping for fabric, but I learned just how fast a quilt can be made. I'd worked out many shortcuts and fast techniques on my one-day orgy of quick quiltmaking, and I also learned more about machine quilting in writing *The Sewing Machine Craft Book* (Prentice Hall, 1981).

So Leslie and I dashed off to the fabric store, figuring out the design and layout on an envelope back, and buying yardage amounts by guesswork. I don't recommend this; therefore, this book contains step-by-step directions for making 13 quilts. Claudia's quilt was a success, too, in spite of our casual approach.

Since then, Leslie, Rosemary, Helen Balmer, Claudia, my sister, my mother, my cousin, other friends, and I (in various groupings) have made many friendship quilts for weddings, birthdays, a retirement, and a baby's birth. In addition to these, this book shows other contemporary and antique friendship quilts made by different groups. I have loved discovering and sharing the history, the designs, the techniques, the friends, and the many curious details about this special kind of quilt.

Friends, I discovered — as you will — turn out to be the essential element of friendship quilts. Experts in some future era may analyze the stitches or the fabrics on your quilt, but you'll always care more about your friend's handmade square and what it means to you.

I hope you have as much fun making these playful quilts as my friends and I have.

Friendship QUILTS
BY HAND AND MACHINE

Introduction

Not many of the things you give to a friend will last for generations, but friendship quilts have that potential. Part of the fun in making a square for a quilt is to imagine who will see it in the future. With most of the blocks done by amateur stitchers, rather than expert quilters, friendship quilts qualify as contemporary folk art. Those that endure the wear and tear of living and loving will eventually become heirlooms.

Handmade quilts of bygone days took endless hours to make. Few of us nowadays are willing to spend weeks, months or years handstitching an entire quilt, especially if it will be given away. Most of the quilts you'll see in this book are a combination of hand and machine sewing, depending on the design, the fabric, the stitchers' skills, and time limitations. Today's stitchers use the sewing machine, the photocopier, the paper cutter, fabric glues, iron-on crayons, anything that helps make a friendship quilt go faster and look delightful.

Contemporary friendship quilts, while often based on earlier ones, have a distinct style all their own. Further, they even vary regionally, with the East, the Midwest and California all having distinctive, recognizable styles.

A friendship quilt provides a way of saving a friend's personality, better than a photograph. Does a photo show who's neat, who's impatient, who's imaginative, who's sentimental? Quilt squares do. A friendship quilt keeps friends together in one place for you to recall, and your descendants to wonder about.

Why Make a Friendship Quilt?

All the good reasons for making these quilts in the 1800s still apply, with even more today. Here are several reasons why you might like to make a friendship quilt:

1. To commemorate an event, such as a wedding, a birth, or a retirement.
2. For the personal touch—a handmade, signed square keeps on saying "Remember me."
3. Group quilts make up faster, and the sewing machine speeds them up even more.
4. To share in tradition; quilting bees never go out of style.
5. To get together with friends—and even make assembling the quilt the excuse for a full-fledged party.
6. A chance to be creative, and to include friends and relatives who may think they aren't creative.

Fig. 1 Louise's Antique Crazy Quilt, made in a style popular from 1875 to 1900, features friends' embroidered signatures on elegant patches.

2

Fig. 2 The Trenton Quilt, 1839, has a single repeat pattern of pieced blocks in reds and white with inked signatures and sayings. Courtesy of Mary Silber.

7. To create a keepsake, as cherished by the recipient's grandchildren decades from now, as it will be by the honoree when first given.

Don't worry that your friends may not be able to sew a square with the exquisite skill of our ancestors (compare Figs. 2 and 3). There are ways to get around this so everyone can participate. Few of the people who contributed squares for the quilts shown throughout this book are expert quilters, but many of their squares are charming. The total effect is what counts.

And that may be what makes this book different from other quilt books.

Fig. 3 One of 24 blocks from Claudia Hall Stroud's friendship quilt, 1981.

3

Of course, all kinds of traditional ways to make friendship quilts are included, but emphasis is on creating your own square or quilt design in your own way. Most friendship quilts aren't meant to win show prizes; they are meant to get your friends together to make a quilt and enjoy the whole process.

How to Use This Book

You won't need to read the whole book to find out what you want to know. The chapters are arranged so that each gives some specific information on technique or organization, and includes a successful friendship quilt as the example. Directions for making these special quilts, from planning to binding, are included. For example, if you want to make a quilt similar to Claudia's wedding quilt, read Chapter 1 on the whole process of making a group friendship quilt, and then follow the directions given for making a quilt like hers. Or find another quilt you like and follow those instructions.

If you like the color scheme and layout, but want to use a different theme or technique, consult the Quilt Chart in the Appendix. It lists the details of all the quilts so you can choose and combine ideas. Use this book like a supermarket, collecting an idea for a theme here, a color scheme there, a sewing technique from another chapter, and a display idea from another.

Lots of people gave me tips on their friendship quilt projects, which I've included to help you design and make your quilt, even including enjoying the quilt party.

Chapter 1

The Whole Process

Claudia's Wedding Quilt

A friendship quilt is a spread of cozy memories made especially for someone from patches sewn by friends, relatives, and neighbors. These quilts may come in many different forms and faces, but they all symbolize and record in a warm visual way the bonds people form with each other.

"The best part of my friendship quilt was opening wedding shower gifts and finding the wonderful squares made by my friends," my daughter Claudia says about her keepsake quilt. "I felt so honored that people took the time to make them for me. I could see by their smiles at the shower people thought 'I'll be so happy for her to see my square'."

Many recipients of quilts made by friends say how awed they felt by the tangible expression of friendship. Mary Silber, noted quilt collector, says "The strength of a friendship quilt is what goes on between the maker and the receiver. Nobody else quite understands the message."

It's true. Plenty of the friends' quilt squares in this book look like pirates' treasure maps with their cryptic symbols, numbers, and images. Nobody seems to care on these homey quilts if others can decipher the message. Ones like "Remember Myrtle Beach" on Peter's Quilt aim for a little mystery. And I couldn't resist sewing a "hidden message" in my block for Claudia's wedding quilt.

Claudia's Quilt, Step-by-Step

The finished quilt was the main goal, but along the way we discovered that doing it was even more fun. We loved getting together to plan, choosing fabrics and colors, discussing ideas for squares, helping some with sewing, and seeing the finished blocks at the party. This cheerful hubbub was the best part and it's what I see in the finished quilt.

By good fortune our method for making Claudia's Quilt worked beautifully (Fig. 1–1). The quilt turned out so well that every new bride in our group wanted one. (And several un-brides like me wanted one, too.) We used the same method over and over to make friends' quilts, with minor changes to fit circumstances.

This chapter takes you through the method step-by-step so you can see how easy it is. Sharing the construction of blocks with so many friends helps the quilt go faster, with no one

Fig. 1–1 Claudia's Wedding Quilt; 24 friends and relatives appliquéd squares in soft colors from melon, gold and off-white, to taupe, khaki, and soft purple.

overburdened. Each new quilt varied a bit, according to owner's tastes, theme, time available to make it, and number of friends to make squares. You can use the basic plan here, with variations to suit your needs and likes. Follow directions for making Claudia's Quilt in detail, or consult other chapters for changes. Look at Louise's Quilt to see why fabric choices are so significant. Read how Lori's color phobias were taken into account, how design makes Peter's Quilt work so well, and how machine appliqué suited the Artists' Quilt. Choose whatever ideas it takes to create your own treasure.

Here's what worked, what didn't, what was fun, and what was funny. We did these steps in any order that came to us, happily bumbling our way through.

1. Select a designer to organize the quilt
2. Choose the occasion
3. Schedule the time
4. List the contributors
5. Decide theme and technique
6. Design the quilt layout
7. Choose related colors
8. Pick suitable fabrics
9. Measure and buy yardage
10. Make the kits
11. Design the invitations
12. Plan the party
13. Assemble the quilt top
14. Finish the quilt
15. Display the quilt

Choose a Designer to Organize the Quilt

Anyone who can organize a project, can sew or knows someone who can, and wants to make a friendship quilt can fill this role. Among our friends, whoever decides to make the quilt is in charge. The quilt designer's job is to plan it and see it through to completion. She controls color, theme, and arrangement of diverse returned blocks to unify the quilt.

For organizational style, I recommend a monarchy over a democracy. Leslie and I decided to be the bosses. Otherwise, we and our friends all have so many opinions, we'd still be having committee meetings. As the quilt bosses—ahem, as quilt designers—we chose colors and fabrics, made up and sent out the kits, helped people make squares when asked, collected and arranged the blocks, and assembled the quilt. Nobody minded carrying out our plans when we asked nicely, listened to their ideas, and offered lots of help.

It's nice but not necessary to have an organized group to make a friendship quilt. All you really need is one or two quilters to do the big job of planning, apportioning fabrics, and assembly, plus a group of friends. On our quilts, whoever was invited to the event got included in the group. It's even possible to do a friendship quilt totally by mail. (For other methods, see Chapter 2.)

Choose the Occasion

Douglas Stroud selected the occasion when he proposed to Claudia. The festive August wedding shower gave people ideas about imagery for their squares, and a specific deadline by which to complete them. At the shower, everyone enjoyed the show-and-tell of each other's squares. I know this spurred them to create more imaginative designs and careful sewing. On later quilts, I found it more difficult to get

Fig. 1–2 Blocks include Brooke Greeson's cat, Helen Balmer's graphic *Hs*, Lois Goodrich's family circle, and mother's sewing machine.

people to participate without the sociability of a party or get-together.

Schedule the Time

Douglas proposed to Claudia on May 19, and this threw all kinds of plans into action for their September 5 wedding. It took until early June to get our plans together for the August bridal shower and to make our way to the fabric store, leaving about a month and a half for the people invited to make their blocks.

Fig. 1–3 Quilt blocks include Joan Jacobi's rabbit cloud, Leslie Masters Villani's acrylic-painted self-portrait, Lindsay Balmer's geometric appliqué, and Elaine Masters' abstract.

Six weeks turned out to be a good length of time for making a block, although the actual construction may take less than a day. With longer time, the packet of fabrics you send will get lost in that pile of mail in the kitchen, and with shorter notice people may have trouble fitting it into their plans.

Our various groups of friends tended to make casual quilts, but some groups go for stricter standards with elaborate techniques. These quilts will take longer to make, possibly a year or more. On the other hand, Julie's Quilt took less than a week, done in a special way (see Chapter 10).

List the Contributors

Our list of square-makers included twenty wedding shower guests, but what about friends and relatives who couldn't come? We added some out-of-towners who we knew would want to make squares: Grandmother Vosburg in Florida, Aunt Lois in Philadelphia, and Claudia's sister-in-law Susie in Pennsylvania.

Before we could lay out a quilt, we needed a count of people who would make squares. Even then, we had to plan a bit loosely because the number kept changing. Two or three people didn't return their completed squares until we offered more help. And some others heard about the quilt and asked to make a square. Ways to cope with adding or subtracting squares are covered in Chapters 3 and 4.

Select Theme and Technique

A look at our list of contributors showed that some were artists, but most were just friends with unknown talents. All were interesting people, so, for a theme, we decided to ask each person to do something personal on the square. We forgot to specifically request names and many only added initials, so ask for signatures. You'll want to know in years to come who JSD was.

We didn't know who sewed and who didn't, so we tried to find an easy technique. We settled on appliqué, the closest thing in sewing to cutting and pasting colored paper, something we all did in grade school. We planned to send swatches of fabric colors and let friends come up with their own designs. For those who needed or wanted help, we offered to appliqué their designs. If you don't want to do this, encourage square-makers to ask other friends for help.

Anyone's square can turn out to be a winner. Claudia's favorites weren't directly related to artistic ability or sewing skills (see details of blocks in Figs. 1–2 through 1–6). We liked some of the most primitive the best. On the finished quilt all the squares went together just fine! On later quilts, we tried other themes and techniques. Pick the one that suits your friends best.

Design the Quilt Layout

By good luck, Leslie and I settled on a square background block of fabric.

Fig. 1–4 Of course, Mrs. MacIntosh showed Macintosh apples on her block, done in machine appliqué with a satin-stitch outline.

Fig. 1–5 Rosemary Squires' block includes her three daughters' couched cord initials, Mary Zdrodowski covered Claudia's "S" with colorful embroidery, Nancy Yaw made traditional gathered circles, and Nancy Stroud hand-appliquéd the Stroud farm.

This sounds too obvious, but when we sent out rectangles for a later quilt, you guessed it: at least one came in vertical even though we specified horizontal. (We made a pillow from it.)

We planned a double-bed size, using a sheet for backing. This dimension, coupled with the number of blocks invited, determined the 12″-square size of the sections and the layout. We didn't know if people would really do their squares, and assumed that only

Fig. 1–6 Photographer Peggy Day hand-appliquéd a cat behind a camera for art director Claudia's quilt.

twenty of the twenty-four sent out would come in. We planned to lay blocks out in five horizontal rows of four each. This left 4″ between each for spacers and 10″ on each edge for the border (see Fig. 1–8). The easiest way to design and lay out a quilt is on graph paper. If you have a full pad of graph paper, try several layouts to see what will work best.

Surprise! For Claudia's quilt all twenty-four squares came in, so we put four on the corners, trimmed to 10″. It pays to keep your plan a bit flexible, since you can never be sure how many squares will be returned.

After wrestling with the size of this quilt, we decided to make later quilts smaller. These big quilts are unwieldy to quilt, expensive to make, and more difficult to display on the wall.

Choose Related Colors

We wanted to surprise Claudia, so we didn't ask her to help choose colors. Leslie did ask her for color ideas for shower gifts and this helped us as quilt planners. Claudia got the only surprise—all the later brides made sure their mothers knew they wanted quilts and in what colors.

Colors create the mood, style, and personality of a quilt. Color is what makes the quilt sing. Potential quilt owners will have strong ideas about what they like. I recommend you consult the honoree or a close friend about colors.

Leslie and I both love colors and are also very picky about the right shades. As you can imagine, it took hours to select eight good colors that we both agreed on, but we had a good time doing it. We chose off-white, light gold, pink, and melon for background squares, picked three muted colors— taupe, khaki, and a light-and-dark taupe print—for spacers and borders, and added a soft purple for accent. These were all muted off-shades, which gave a subtle effect. If you prefer a more scenic quilt, plan greater contrast in stronger colors.

Don't be surprised if you spend longer than you expect in the fabric store choosing the right colors. This is the most important decision about the quilt. (For extensive information about color, see Chapter 5.)

Pick Suitable Fabrics

Leslie and I planned to machine sew the entire quilt, so we could choose from a wide range of fabrics. We limited the weave and fiber content so we wouldn't get a let's-throw-in-the-kitchen-sink look. We considered all kinds of cotton-polyester fabrics searching for just the right colors.

The nice, firm, medium-weight broadcloth we chose would be great for machine stitching, but hard to ply a hand needle through. The soft cotton print we picked would be ideal for hand sewing, but a bit flimsy for machine stitching. A heavier, more stable background fabric is less apt to pucker and shift when satin-stitch appliqué pieces are added. Read Chapter 6 for some ideas on coping with these problems, so you can choose suitable fabrics for your quilt based on the way you plan to stitch and quilt it.

Note that a quilt this size can become expensive: 15 yards of fabric plus the sheet and the batting cost over $60 five years ago (more now), and the postage, photocopying of the directions, envelopes, invitations, and stamps added up, too. We four friends split the quilt and party costs, but be sure to allocate your expenses when you plan the quilt.

Measure and Buy the Yardage

When we had settled on colors and fabrics, I made little drawings to see how the squares, spacers, intersections, borders, and additional pieces would fit on various widths of fabric. You'll save time if you lay out your quilt on graph paper before arriving at the store. Don't forget to add seam allowances to each piece for estimating yardage needed.

It helps to use a hand calculator to figure yardage. Decide which pieces will be made in which colors and compute the amounts you'll need. You can make notes on your layout diagram to make sure you have included everything.

With four different background colors, we divided the yardage needed for squares by four, and then added some for the appliqué pieces. We had no idea how much people would need for appliqués, so we decided to send them pieces of each color, measuring from about 6" square to 5" × 10". This general size turns out to be fine for most quilts. Not all appliqué pieces need be the same dimensions.

Specific materials for Claudia's Quilt appear in the profile at the end of this chapter. For general information on measuring and laying out pieces for cutting, fabric widths, and amounts to buy, see Chapter 3. Be sure to make up your kits right away, in case you need to return to the store for more fabric.

Prepare the Kits

Our kits included a 13" fabric background square, a swatch of each of the colors, and directions on how to make the square. We also tucked in an invitation to the shower.

I cut the fabrics into squares and appliqué swatches. After snipping, ripping and clipping, I was surrounded by piles of fabrics, one with twenty-four background fabric squares and eight with twenty-four pieces of each color. And I saved extra fabric in case of problems.

Leslie and I assembled the kits. In each kit we put one of the four background colors, and the other seven colors of fabric swatches. Leslie wrapped the fabric swatches in netting and tied them with a ribbon. She can make everything look like a present, no matter how ordinary. She tucked these, along with the shower invitation, into a 6″ × 9″ envelope, and then drew marker designs on the outside.

Include whatever people will need in your kits. Our background fabric was firm enough for machine sewing, but on a later quilt we included iron-on backing to stabilize a very soft fabric. For embroidery kits, you may want to include embroidery floss or yarns. The more materials you include in the quilt, the fewer surprises you'll get on the returned block.

Design the Invitation

Our party invitation had to do two things: invite people to the shower and involve them in the friendship quilt. We sent a cute commercial invitation to the shower (with RSVP) to post on their bulletin boards. Our invitation to join in the friendship quilt filled a standard typing page (Fig. 1–7). We added a border of quilt square drawings, and had it photocopied. To brighten the plain white, we colored some of the design with marking pens.

Instructions included every detail we could think of for making the square. On later quilts, we included even more specifics. No matter, instructions never tell everything someone wants to know; put your phone number and address on, so people can ask for clarification. Sample invita-

tions are included for several of the quilts; use ours or create your own, but be sure your invitations convey contagious enthusiasm.

Plan the Party

Rosemary planned a number of playful shower games. Helen and Rosemary brought marvelous party food, and Leslie decorated her house with pink frills, including a sheet on the wall to pin up the quilt squares.

Claudia was overwhelmed with surprise and delight when gifts were opened and the squares revealed. Of course, several people demurred, "You don't need to use mine," and "I'm not an artist," but Claudia loved them all, knowing the effort put into them.

By the time Julie got married, we dispensed with the shower games and devoted the entire day, except for lunch and gifts, to making the squares by stenciling with fabric paints. (For more details, see Chapter 10.)

Part of the fun is in seeing what other contributors did, and quilts made by mail miss this chance for show-and-tell. People often send notes with their returned squares. Keep all notes in an envelope and give them to the honoree along with the quilts. (It's nice to send a photo of the finished quilt to each participant, too.)

Assemble the Quilt Top

Don't hesitate to remind laggards that you need their squares: Some people lack the confidence to complete them and will appreciate your offer of help. Once all the squares have arrived, you can begin to arrange them.

Please join us in making a
Friendship Quilt for
_ _ _ _ _ _ _ _ _ _ _

To celebrate the
_ _ _ _ _ _ _ _ _ _ _
on _ _ _ _ _ _ _ _ _ _ _

Enclosed please find a
background square
and several colors of
fabric so you can - - - →

Appliqué a design
showing something
that will remind the
new quilt owner
of YOU - - →

Hand or machine sew your
square ~ add embroidery
if you wish, and leave a
one inch border for seaming
the quilt together . . . _ _ _ →

Don't forget to
include your name
on the square so
you'll always be
remembered.

Please return your square
to _ _ _ _ _ _ _ _ _ _
by _ _ _ _ _ _ _ _ _ _

Thanks so much...
*
*
*
*
*

Fig. 1–7 Photocopy this invitation for Claudia's quilt, or use Peter's,
Amy's, Kim's, or Carolyn's. Cover any unwanted words with your own,
written on white paper. Add color with markers or crayons.

Since the squares for Claudia's Quilt were so individual, I wondered at first sight if they would all go together on the same quilt. It took quite awhile to balance them for best effect, shifting blocks from one spot to another. I laid them out on the floor, so I could stand on a chair to get an overall view. (For assistance in arranging blocks, see Chapter 11.)

Finish the Quilt

Leslie and I made this quilt like a comforter since we planned to machine quilt it. This means we laid the face and backing, right sides together, with the filler on top, and sewed around three edges. Then we turned the whole thing right-side out and closed the open edge. Later, Leslie machine quilted the layers.

This technique is a life saver. So many friendship quilts languish half-finished because the quilting part takes forever. Use my "comforter style" technique and the quilt looks finished before it is quilted. You (or someone) can quilt at leisure. And don't worry about doing exhibition quality solid quilting. These quilts look best with minimal quilting.

Those of you who must have exquisite quilting can sandwich the layers together, hand quilt them on a frame or hoop, and then finish the edge with binding. These methods and others are covered in more detail in Chapter 12.

Plan for Display

Leslie ran her sewing machine like a runaway truck down a hill and finished the quilt before the wedding. Claudia proudly showed it to everyone, often explaining the significance of the cryptic squares. "The basket of apples in the corner is from Mrs. MacIntosh, my grandmother sewed her cat, Margo made herself on the vacation we shared."

Quilts, as large and colorful as they are, make a wonderful focal point in a room. Owners often plan the room around them. It is best to hang quilts out of the direct sunlight, since this will surely fade the colors and destroy the fabric over a period of time. Claudia uses hers on the guest room bed. It's too big to hang easily on the wall. For more information on the display and care of friendship quilts, see Chapter 13.

The Gift of Friendship

The most special quality about a friendship quilt is the gift of time and self. Valuable as linens, crystal, and china given at a shower are, the time and creativity given by a friend to make a square is priceless. Claudia and I look over her quilt and find ourselves smiling, happy to have these friends. You'll get the same pleasure "mothering" a quilt through to completion as Leslie and I did . . . do.

Claudia's Wedding Quilt

QUILT PROFILE

OCCASION: The wedding of Claudia Hall and Douglas Stroud (September, 1981).

GROUP: Friends and relatives

QUILT DESIGNERS: Leslie Masters Villani and Carolyn Vosburg Hall.

ORGANIZATION: Kits containing a background fabric square and swatches of seven appliqué colors were sent to wedding shower guests to complete and bring to the shower.

THEME: Shared personal scenes.

TECHNIQUE: Completed blocks include appliqué by hand and machine, pieced blocks, machine embroidery, hand embroidery, and added ribbons, buttons, laces and trims. Imagery includes Grandmother Vosburg's fat grey Persian cat, Brooke Greeson's comical cat, and gallery owner Nancy Yaw's 1930s-style gathered circles. Rosemary gave advice to newly marrieds under a leaf, Helen made *H*s, and Leslie painted a self portrait. Photographer Peggy Day formed her fabric to create a dimensional camera with a covered circle for the lens. Aunt Lois made a family circle. Mary Z. embellished an S monogram with colorful hand embroidery.

TIME: Kits went out in June, for an August wedding shower.

SIZE: 80″ wide × 96″ long

BLOCKS: Twenty-four blocks, each 12″ square

LAYOUT: Four blocks across, five rows; four 10″ blocks in the 10″ border corners; 4″ spacers (sashing); 4″-square intersections

COLORS: White, light gold, pink, melon, purple, khaki, taupe, and taupe print.

YARDAGE TOTAL: 14¾ yards of 45″-wide fabrics, plus a queen-size sheet.

FABRIC: Cotton and poly/cotton broadcloths.

FILLER: Polyester fiberfill bonded batting.

QUILTING METHOD: Machine quilted, comforter style (see Chapter 12).

DISPLAY: Claudia uses the quilt on her antique Hall family bed for guests.

MATERIALS

(Buy extra fabric for safety margin)

Background squares: twenty-four 14″ squares in pink, melon, light gold , white (plus extra squares)

Appliqué pieces: eighteen pieces, each about 7″ × 9″ in all eight colors

Background and appliqué:

White fabric	2	yards
Pink fabric	2	yards
Melon fabric	2	yards
Light gold fabric	2	yards

Border: sides, two strips 12″ × 78″; top and bottom, two strips 12″ × 62″ taupe print (plus appliqué) — 2⅔ yards

Sashing: thirty-one pieces, 6″ × 14″ khaki (plus appliqué) — 2¾ yards

Intersections: twelve pieces, 6″ square taupe (plus appliqué) — 1⅓ yards

Total — 14¾ yards

Backing: queen-size sheet, trimmed to 82″ × 98″: 6 sq. yards

Filler: 81″ × 96″ bonded fiberfill batting

Other supplies: assorted harmonizing colors of machine sewing and hand embroidery threads; sewing machine; safety pins; 2″ quilting pins; 24″ quilting hoop

PROCEDURES

1. Assemble the fabrics and supplies. Cut out the pieces, which include 1″ seam allowances (most quilts include a ½″ seam allowance. Follow Fig. 1–8 for the layout of the quilt.

2. Assemble twenty-four kits, including one of the four background colors, seven of the eight appliqué colors (excluding background), and directions for making the squares (see invitation diagram).

3. Inspect the squares. We were impressed with what our friends did on their blocks. They had used machine and hand appliqué, machine and hand embroidery, pieced patchwork patterns, folded and tucked fabrics, gathered fabrics, acrylic painted fabric, and glued-on sequins, which we replaced for the sake of washability with buttons and metallic gold fabric. (For details on these techniques, see Chapters 6, 7, 8, 9, and 10.)

Some squares needed a little help. When a block was badly puckered, I removed the stitching with a seam ripper and resewed it using machine satin stitch. If friends had no time or incli-

18

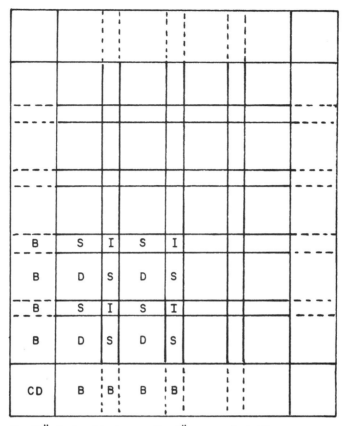

D: 12" design blocks   S: 4" spacer in lattice
B: 10" borders   I: 4" square intersections
CD: 10" design blocks

Fig. 1–8 Claudia's Wedding Quilt layout diagram, 80″ × 96″.

nation to sew, they pinned on a design and Leslie or I sewed it for them. If the square looked too bare, we added a ribbon border. If no name was included, I free-motion machine stitched it.

4. Assemble the squares, sashing, intersections and border into a quilt face (for details, see Chapter 11). For assembling the layers, quilting, and finishing, see details in Chapter 12.

Chapter 2

Eight Ways to Organize a Quilt
The Minister's Retirement Quilt

Remember when Mickey Rooney bounced around in a movie, shouting to Judy Garland and their pals, "Hey, gang. Let's put on a show!" And then they'd come up with a smash Hollywood review, a little hay-seedy around the edges to show they were just ordinary kids.

Well, that's the exuberant way many friendship quilts are made. "Hey, gang, let's make a friendship quilt!" For 150 years people have been putting together these wonderful productions, and you can too.

The many ways of organizing a friendship quilt will be discussed later in this chapter, but first let's review a little history of early American quilts, and discuss the many elements, using the one made for Rev. Bob Marshall by members of his congregation as our example.

Historic Friendship Quilts

When the earliest known friendship quilts appeared in the 1830s, signatures were inscribed in flowing penmanship in ink, and later stitched in intricate hand embroidery on each friend's square or patch. The true friendship quilt was made of pieced blocks in homey scraps of saved fabrics. These quilts could not be washed because of the inked signatures.

During the same era, an appliquéd quilt of planned color and design with signatures was called an album quilt (Fig. 2–2). Autograph albums as "repositories of mementos of early affections" had been popular before 1835. The idea of immortalizing friendships flowed over to quilts with the invention of an ink that would not destroy the fabrics.

The form of the quilts changed over the years. In the 1880s, signed crazy quilts in elegant fabrics were all the vogue. The names changed too; these quilts were variously called friendship quilts, album quilts, signature quilts and name quilts. Our contemporary versions are different again, but the main aim—to honor friendships—has not changed.

Making the Minister's Quilt

When Bob Marshall, the minister at the Unitarian Church in Birmingham, Michigan, planned to retire in 1984, the church Alliance group decided to produce a friendship quilt for him. Elaine Morse, one of the organizers,

Fig. 2–1 The Minister's Retirement Quilt, made for Rev. Bob Marshall by eighty members of his Unitarian congregation. Dark green and red borders and lattice surround blocks in all colors and fabrics.

21

Fig. 2–2 Detail of an inked signature on the Trenton Quilt, dated March 6, 1839, one of the earliest friendship quilts known.

told me what a great time they had getting all those independent-minded Unitarians to create quilt blocks.

Quilt blocks had to be small, 6″ square, since eighty people or more wanted to be included (Fig. 2–1). Some people made their designs at home, but many attended get-togethers at the church to work on their squares, to chat, and to see what others were doing. Experienced stitchers helped others to carry out their ideas.

It's no wonder this kind of get-together is called a quilting bee. The Unitarian group sounded like any other group of quilters, a happy hive of buzzing bees going about their work in energetic harmony. To make a quilt with as many participants as this one, see the quilt profile at the end of the chapter.

The Four Elements of a Friendship Quilt

Both old and new friendship quilts always have four components: (1) An honoree and event are chosen; (2) a theme is selected; (3) a group of people are asked to take part; and (4) a design for the quilt is decided upon.

These decisions can be made in any order; there's no special magic in the sequence. Often, a specific event triggers the decision to make a friendship quilt, so let's start with that.

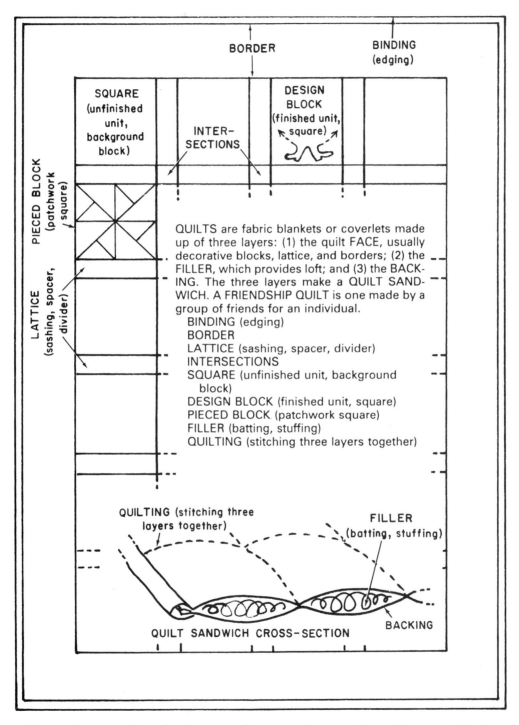

BORDER

BINDING (edging)

SQUARE (unfinished unit, background block)

INTER-SECTIONS

DESIGN BLOCK (finished unit, square)

PIECED BLOCK (patchwork square)

LATTICE (sashing, spacer, divider)

QUILTS are fabric blankets or coverlets made up of three layers: (1) the quilt FACE, usually decorative blocks, lattice, and borders; (2) the FILLER, which provides loft; and (3) the BACK-ING. The three layers make a QUILT SAND-WICH. A FRIENDSHIP QUILT is one made by a group of friends for an individual.

BINDING (edging)
BORDER
LATTICE (sashing, spacer, divider)
INTERSECTIONS
SQUARE (unfinished unit, background block)
DESIGN BLOCK (finished unit, square)
PIECED BLOCK (patchwork square)
FILLER (batting, stuffing)
QUILTING (stitching three layers together)

QUILTING (stitching three layers together)

FILLER (batting, stuffing)

BACKING

QUILT SANDWICH CROSS-SECTION

Fig. 2–3 Anatomy of a quilt. Some parts have several names; the one I use most often is given first, with others in parentheses.

Honoree/Event

Friendship quilts may commemorate any event or occasion: At least seven of the quilts in this book celebrate weddings; some are for babies or children, such as Janet's baby shower quilt and my grandchild Hattie's First Birthday Quilt. Perhaps your parents are having a fiftieth anniversary. Or your best friend is turning 40. You can make a quilt for any special event—a graduation, a good-bye quilt for a friend moving away, your city's centennial.

Church groups often use this means to honor a pastor upon retirement or marriage—or to raise money for the church. Many groups these days make a quilt to raffle to raise money for an art association, church, or peace group. I'm in favor of this delightful idea, but such group quilts may lack the personal elements of a friendship quilt. On the other hand, maybe not: the Idaho Peace Quilt is being sent to various senators to use for a night, and may even go to Russian politicians. The women who made it hope the warmth and caring that went into it will be felt by all who come in contact with the quilt.

If no special event occurs conveniently (and your friends haven't taken up your hints), make a friendship quilt for yourself. I did, and I love it (see Chapter 10). An honoree will probably be pleased to be asked to make a block for his or her quilt, too, unless a surprise is planned.

Theme

The theme of a quilt can be the same as its reason for creation. For example, over the years both old quilts and new have featured patriotic themes. Several of these quilts hang in former President Gerald Ford's Library on the University of Michigan campus. The Parkview High School students in Little Rock, Arkansas, made a delightful one in the form of an American flag in 1976 (see color section).

The Bicentennial also inspired many communities to assemble large groups to make historic quilts featuring scenes of their towns (Fig. 2–4). People delight in the quilts' carefully documented scenes of familiar environs (see the Birmingham Quilt, Chapter 13).

You can also make a quilt of scenes

Fig. 2–4 A block from the Birmingham Bicentennial Quilt, 1976, shows hand-appliquéd figures marching in a parade.

24

dear to you (or the honoree) as a theme: houses, portraits of friends, fabrics from special clothing, garden flowers, pets, clever sayings, important symbols, favorite toys, or holiday mementos.

The Group

Sometimes it's a special group of friends who provide the inspiration to make a quilt. My artist friends made one of my favorites, shown in Chapter 8. And the children's classes at the Birmingham Bloomfield Art Association (Michigan) contributed to the delightful Kids' Quilt in Chapter 10. Any group might decide to stitch a quilt—a family, neighborhood friends, a club, the PTA, the Girl Scouts, or a church group.

In 1902, the ladies of the Presbyterian Church in Birmingham, Michigan, made a raffle quilt. Plain white background squares were raffled off to church members to sign and embroider. Their friends contributed signatures too. The unfinished quilt top was discovered recently in Mrs. Allen's attic and returned to the church for quilting. It is now displayed in the church archive room.

Design and Technique

Most of the quilts shown in this book are appliquéd on background squares and feature added embroidery, especially for the signatures. The colors chosen, the imagery on the squares and the arrangement of the squares all vary. You can choose from many techniques, including (but not limited to) counted cross stitch (Mary's Quilt, Chapter 10), crayon transfer (Kids' Quilt, Chapter 10), stenciling or textile painting (Julie's Quilt, Chapter 10), pieced blocks (Hattie's Quilt, Chapter 7), or embroidery (Amy's Quilt, Chapter 9).

Eight Great Managing Methods

Making a friendship quilt takes a different sort of planning than a one-person effort. It's the difference between cooking the entire Thanksgiving dinner by yourself and inviting all the family and friends for a potluck. The secret to success is planning ahead. You, as chief cook, make the major choices. Friends who would never make a whole quilt will love making one square.

Each quilt needs a "chief cook" that I call the quilt designer, or quilt mother. You need not have an organized group; all you really need is at least one person to do the big job of planning, selecting and apportioning fabrics, and assembling, and a group of willing friends. You, as the quilt designer, can do a minimum of planning, or you can specify most of the details. Here are eight very different ways to manage and organize a quilt projects.

Rotating Quilt Mothers in a Permanent Group

Linda Lowman Barnett, who lives in a remote area of California, belongs to the Greenwood Quilter's Group. They began making baby quilts for pregnant members about ten years ago, and now make them for each member in turn. They meet regularly to plan, ply their needles, and socialize.

In "Threads" magazine Oct/Nov 1986, Linda tells how her group, lead-

Fig. 2–5 Many techniques were used on the Minister's Retirement Quilt: hand embroidery, hand and machine appliqué, and counted cross-stitch (the Focus Hope hands by Rebecca Pedersen).

erless and democratic in format, chooses a quilt mother for each new quilt. The quilt mother confers with the honoree, chooses the theme, size and colors, and moves the quilt along. She also must decide which squares are acceptable.

The "Anything Goes" Approach

Elaine Morse, who helped organize the Unitarian Church members for Bob Marshall's Retirement Quilt, allowed the greatest latitude, simply asking members to contribute 6"-square blocks. Eighty squares came back with every kind of technique, fabric and color in evidence (see Figs. 2–5 through 2–7 for some idea of the variety). Squares were appliquéd, embroidered, pieced, and painted, and included a jeans pocket with handkerchief, a rope, metal rings, buttons and commercial patches.

"Well, we are Unitarians, you know," Elaine says. "Nobody likes being told what to do."

Fig. 2–6 More unusual sewing techniques appear on the Minister's Retirement Quilt: couched rope, a type of reverse appliqué, a pen drawing, and commercial letters and patches.

This leads to marvelous diversity, and not a few problems. Some blocks had seam allowances; some did not. This free-wheeling way of collecting squares takes an innovative "chief cook" or a good committee to assemble the quilt successfully.

The Quilting Bee

In one form of traditional friendship quilting bee, each participant brought her own selection of scraps, while the hostess provided each person with a background square. Fingers and tongues flew all afternoon, as each was supposed to begin and complete her square by the party's end. No doubt they offered each other opinions on color and fabric choices. For a modern-day version of the quilting bee, see Julie's Quilt, Chapter 10.

Mailing Background Squares

For some of the quilts shown, the background fabric squares were speci-

Fig. 2–7 Some families painted designs, others appliquéd or embroidered their blocks, but how about the jeans pocket?

fied by the quilt designer and mailed to those who would attend (usually a wedding shower). Friends decorated these squares at home and brought them to the party. Some people accepted the hostess's offer to sew for them and provided sketches, cut out pieces, or only signed their names. Amy's Quilt in Chapter 9 was made this way. Peter's Quilt in Chapter 3 was made completely by mail, with kits sent out and finished blocks returned by post.

Partly Completed Squares

Since we didn't know who could (or who would) sew a block, for Kim's Quilt (Chapter 4) we sent our background squares with a large heart already machine appliquéd in the center. Shower guests embellished each heart in their own ways, adding embroidery, lace, buttons and bows. They were more imaginative than we ever dreamed.

Adding Signatures to Finished Blocks

For Hattie's Quilt, I pieced the patchwork blocks and Hattie's mom requested signatures from friends to appliqué on plain areas of the blocks. I thought this was cheating until I discovered that most of the earliest friendship quilts were made this way. Patterns for these blocks, including the traditional "Album Block" and Hattie's own newly designed block, "Hattie's Hat," are given in Chapter 7.

Exchanging Blocks

Many quilters exchange completed, pieced blocks for their own friendship quilts, and have been doing this for generations. Not only do they build a delightful quilt block-by-block, but they learn how to make new blocks, and can experiment with original patterns for other quilters.

Janet M. Clark gives some practical advice on exchanging blocks in the "Quilter's Newsletter" magazine, Nov/Dec 1986. She urges that quilters be specific in their requests, listing size, color, construction requirements, and perhaps even providing fabric and a pattern. Don't ask for unusual or elaborate results, she advises, unless you know your trading partner can and will do it. Offer a block in return, promptly. Be sure to thank the block makers. She also advises that, if you are providing a requested block, you don't add weird details. If you cannot comply with the request, send a note to say so.

Sending Kits and Instructions

My friends and I discovered that the most successful method of making quilts is to send a kit, as we did for Claudia's Quilt (Chapter 1). This kit included the background fabric squares, an assortment of coordinated fabric swatches for appliqués, and directions on how to proceed. This controlled the color range, fabric selection, and size. We did several other quilts this way, and most of the instructions in the book are based on this method.

One of these methods should work for you. Or you may be able to combine ideas from more than one technique. Be sure to have meetings to solicit ideas from contributors, too.

A word of wisdom: Remember that you are working with a big group of people, all with minds of their own. Some will disregard your instructions, fail to read them, or come up with "better" ideas. You'll get back some surprises. Be prepared and treat this possibility with good humor. I've learned to look forward to it.

The Minister's Retirement Quilt

QUILT PROFILE

OCCASION: To honor Bob Marshall, retiring minister of the Birmingham, Michigan, Unitarian Church in 1984.

GROUP: Eighty-plus church members contributed squares or helped in some manner. The Alliance provided funding.

QUILT DESIGNERS: Elaine Morse, Judy Amir, and Nancy Pilsner-Doughty.

ORGANIZATION: Church members were simply requested to make a 6″ block with seam allowance, any color, any technique.

THEME: Bob notes that each block had "some connection between me and the person"—a green thumb from the garden committee, for example. Contributors sent notes explaining their squares. Arlene and Ron Frederick said, "The design for this square was originally created by Norbert Capek, Ron's grandfather. Capek founded the Unitarian Church in Czechoslovakia, for which he ultimately died a victim of the Nazi regime. He was also creator of the "Flower Celebration," which has become a June tradition at BUC."

TECHNIQUE: "Anything goes" style. Contributors did whatever they pleased on any kind of block. The assortment of techniques included appliqué, cross stitch, embroidery, couching of added materials, and painting.

TIME: The quilt took about 9 months to make.

SIZE: 69½″ wide × 84½″ long

BLOCK SIZE: 6″ square. Be sure to request a 6″ block with an *added seam allowance of 1″ all around to total an 8″-square block.*

COLORS: Contributors' blocks arrived in all colors. The strong dark green spacers, border, and bindings unified them. Added borders of dark green print and green-and-white gingham kept the detailing in small scale. Red intersections highlighted the all-over pattern.

LAYOUT: Eighty 6″-square blocks, arranged with eight blocks across in ten rows; 1½″ sashing; 1½″-square intersections; a four-part border, including ½″ binding on edges, 2½″ dark green border band, 1¾″ gingham border band.

FABRICS: Contributors used a wide assortment of fabrics. Most are plain weave cottons. Several counted cross-stitch squares are done on Aida cloth. Many squares show embroidered symbols or initials.

YARDAGE: 12¾ yards.

FILLER: Polyester batting.

QUILTING METHOD: The completed quilt face was sent to the Grassroots Co-op in Lost Creek, Kentucky, for quilting. It was stretched on a quilting frame and quilted with dark green thread in overlapping circles around squares and scallop designs on the edges at about 3" intervals. (This quantity of quilting "draws in" the fabric and puffs up the blocks, a charming effect if that's what you want to achieve.)

DISPLAY: Rev. Marshall said the quilt presentation was an overwhelming surprise. The quilt is now on display at the church, the centerpiece of a quilt show.

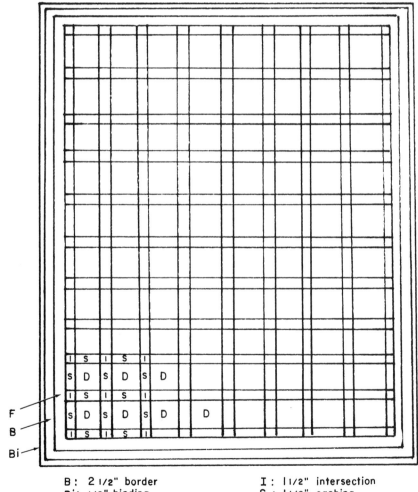

B : 2 1/2" border   I : 1 1/2" intersection
Bi : 1/2" binding   S : 1 1/2" sashing
F : 1 3/4" frame   D : 6" design block

Fig. 2–8 Diagram for the Minister's Retirement Quilt, 69½" × 84½".

MATERIALS

(Buy extra fabric for safety margin)

Design blocks: eighty blocks, 8″ squares	3⅝ yards
Border binding and spacers: dark green	3⅛ yards
Border binding: 3″ × 9 yards	
First border band: 3½″ × 9 yards	
Spacers: 142 pieces, 2½″ × 7″	
Second border band: 2¾″ × 9 yards, gingham	⅔ yard
Intersections: sixty-five 2½″ squares, red cotton	⅓ yard
Backing: two pieces 35¾″ × 85½″, calico	5　yards
Total	13　yards

Filler: 71″ × 86″ bonded polyester batting
Other supplies: dark green sewing thread; scissors; needle; quilting
   frame or 24″ hoop; 2″ quilting pins; safety pins

PROCEDURES

1. Yardage is based on 45″-wide fabric; dimensions include ½″ seam allowances, except blocks, which have 1″ seam allowances. Assemble fabrics and supplies, and cut the layout in Fig. 2–8.

2. To assemble the blocks, sashes and borders, see Chapter 11. Refer to Chapter 12 for detailed instructions on assembling and quilting the top, backing, and batting.

Chapter 3

Design and Layout Planning
Peter's Wedding Quilt

Before friends can do their part on a friendship quilt, the quilt designer has to plan and lay out the quilt. This chapter helps you make the necessary design decisions on every aspect, gives information about standard quilt and bed sizes, and shows how to lay out and compute yardage for fabrics. We'll use Peter's Quilt, begun when he became engaged to Sandy, as the example.

Enthusiasm. That's what shines through when you see Peter's Quilt. It bubbles with exuberance and that's not surprising: Peter and Sandy have an exuberant bunch of friends and relatives. Peter's mother, Lois, the Pied Piper of Home Economics, makes her high school classes so beguiling that she has as many male as female students. And his grandmother paddles her own canoe at age 80. Both were instrumental in planning the quilt and selecting fabrics. While the three of us were in the fabric store, forty bolts of fabric were falling off our carts as we asked each other, "What are Peter and Sandy's favorite colors?" "What will their friends be able to make?" "What fabrics do we need to express our idea?"

Every artist asks herself similar questions about concept, technique, function, form, color, materials, size,

cost and more, whether consciously or not, when planning an artwork. A group of designers planning a new product would confer on like points. Answering these questions is the process of design.

Chatting back and forth in the fabric store didn't seem like an intellectual process at the time. "Say, I like these country colors." "Me, too!" "How many colors do you suppose we need?" "Well, for people they'll need a peachy or flesh tone, and blue for sky and water, green for grass. And a warm golden color, since yellow is too light against white."

"I liked the dark border on the teddy bear quilt you made," Lois said. I agreed that it did make the light squares stand out. We unreeled a dark-brown print next to the pile of fabric bolts we'd chosen to see how they looked together. So far, we'd get a group of fabric colors together, change one, and then have to change the whole bunch. Remember that the fabrics you choose affect the cost, and the cost affects size and therefore amounts of fabric. Like comparing colors, all the design decisions made relate to each other. Make one choice and it helps to make the rest of them.

Mom liked the square Lois had made

Fig. 3–1 Peter's Quilt celebrates the wedding of Sandy Arner and Peter Goodrich in 1984. "Country colors" dominate: off-white background squares, muted green, blue, rusty red and gold print appliqué pieces, and a brown tiny print border.

for Claudia's Quilt. "What are you going to make for Peter's?"

"His old scruffy cat, Tigger. He can't take her with him, but this way he can." And so the theme was decided: people would make favorite things or recall shared times with Sandy and Peter. We determined a size—not too big for a wall hanging; a technique—appliquéd squares; and a time span—to be finished by the wedding day. If this seems pretty causal, we had made quite a few quilts by then.

Planning the Quilt

Quilts are much like paintings. They consist of coordinated colors, arranged in a pleasing design, and enhanced by texture. A good painting is more than decoration, and so, in its own way, is a friendship quilt. Peter and Sandy agree that their quilt gives visual delight to their surroundings.

All that artists know about making good paintings can be useful to you in designing quilts. These design principles were developed to help analyze and plan an artwork. Any good book on design or painting can give you extensive information on color theory, light and dark values, arrangement of shapes and other design concepts.

You can also learn most of this by doing. Every time you make a quilt, you experiment with color relationships, arrangement of shape, and textures. As you create (and afterward) you ask yourself: What worked? What didn't? Why? This is how to learn the design process.

The accompanying, simplified chart lists elements to manipulate in order to achieve various effects.

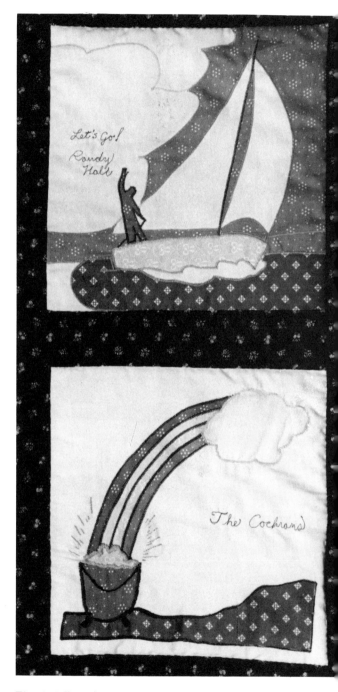

Fig. 3–2 Peter's cousin (my son) Randall Hall waves from a machine-appliquéd sailboat. The Cochrans made a rainbow with a pot of gold for good luck on their square.

35

Elements	Changes	Results
Shape	Color	Harmony
Line	Texture	Balance
Volume	Repetition	Emphasis
	Variation	Movement
	Contrast	Rhythm
	Scale	Order
	Proportion	

Here's how it works. Quilt shapes, whether random appliqué pieces or geometric patchwork pieces, can be varied by all seven ways in the second column (and others). For example, repeated shapes establish a *rhythm*. Bright red shapes are *emphatic*. Large shapes contrast with small shapes for *balance*. Embroidered *lines* embellish shapes in a variety of ways. *Volume,* the dimension created by quilting stitches, gives *texture* to the surface.

Typical friendship quilts achieve *harmony* through repetition of the same-sized blocks and through a controlled color scheme. This helps maintain order on a quilt where many different people create the blocks. The sashing which frames the blocks provides a rhythmic pattern that holds the quilt design together, no matter how dissimilar the squares. (Within limits—if one square contrasts too much, you're in trouble.) Crazy quilts appear to vary from this pattern, but they too are made in blocks. Within the blocks, small-sized patches in repeated warm colors give an all-over harmony. When studying quilts and paintings, try to decide how the design elements were

Fig. 3–3 Peter's grandmother, Doris Vosburg, hand-stitched Rosie on the door step. Peter's Mother, Lois Goodrich, duplicated her Pennsylvania Dutch wedding plate that he has always liked.

manipulated. Try to do the same things yourself.

Choices for Peter's Quilt

Designing the quilt means exercising control over the design elements to varying degrees. The more decisions we made about Peter and Sandy's quilt, the less left to chance. How we made these choices affected the entire project. For example:

- We provided fabrics, saving participants the need to shop for their own and controlling the colors and fiber content of the quilt.
- The theme of shared memories gave square-makers a starting point for ideas.
- We chose a good range of colors so contributors could create a wide variety of scenes.
- Good directions on how to appliqué a square, and what size, helped people know how to proceed and insured that our layout would work.
- Saying we planned to show it at the wedding spurred participants to return finished squares on time.

And what if we didn't make choices?

- Square makers might use unusual fabrics in strange colors. (For some quilts, this may be what you want; see the Minister's Retirement Quilt in Chapter 2 for a charming example. But remember that even deciding not to be specific is a decision.)
- Returned squares might be any size, shape, or fabric, making it difficult to fit the pieces into a quilt.

Fig. 3–4 There by the pool is Tigger, Peter's beloved cat; the next door neighbor's animals keep him company on the block above.

You are invited to make a friendship QUILT SQUARE

for _____

to celebrate _____

on _____

   Please design something showing a shared memory on the fabric background square enclosed. Leave a half-inch border all around for assembling the quilt. Include your name as part of your design.

   The appliqué kit also includes fabric patches for your design. You can hem pieces, sew them on by hand, and decorate with embroidery. Or cut pieces out, use a glue-baste stick to hold them down, and machine sew them in place. Use backing fabric, backing paper, and/ or a machine embroidery hoop to keep your stitches from puckering the fabric. Add embroidery or other washable trim, in these same colors, if you wish.

   S.O.S. Call or write if you want to confer. If you haven't time or don't sew, return your fabrics and your design and I'll complete it for you.

   Send your block back by _____
so the quilt will be ready for _____
Use the addressed and stamped envelope enclosed.

Thanks for joining this keepsake quilt.

_____

_____

_____

Fig. 3–5 Invitation for Peter's Quilt.

- You may get back a counted-cross-stitch square, when all the rest are appliquéd.
- You may get nothing back, as people are still trying to decide what to do.

Don't scoff. All this—and more—has happened on one quilt or another. Now I look forward to the surprises. This leads, of course, to the second half of the design process: putting together the squares you get back. See Chapter 11 for suggestions on handling "surprises," but keep in mind the elements of design, especially balance, from the beginning. You need to control some of these elements to have a successful quilt.

Make a photocopy of the checklist as a reminder of decisions to be made in planning a group quilt. Use the blanks to write in your own decisions. Doing this may keep you from forgetting something. Add more points to consider if needed. Each chapter has a Quilt Profile which you can compare to the photographs to see how each decision affected the results.

Dimensions and Layout

Determining Overall Size

After you've made a queen-sized friendship quilt, the idea of making one the size of an afghan or wall hanging will look better and better. Struggling with one of these king or queen-

sized babies is like trying to put an inflated life raft back in the bag. While a quilt need not fit a bed specifically, it should be a usable size.

To figure overall size, put a blanket or sheet on the bed and drape or fold the edges to allow for the amount of drop you want. Usually the drop covers the mattress edges, while the dust ruffle covers the box spring to the floor. If you want your quilt to cover the pillow, push a fold at the pillow base and spread the sheet over the pillow; remember that some of the design will be lost in the fold.

To see how the size and number of blocks you plan to use fit, lay cut-to-size colored paper or newspaper blocks on the sheet. When the folded and tucked sheet looks the size you want your quilt to be, measure it for width and length.

To compute rather than measure, standard bed sizes are given in the accompanying chart. For example, single beds are 38″ wide and 75″ long. Add a 10″ drop (or whatever you want) at each side and one end. The quilt could measure, rounded off, 60″ wide by 84″ long—or 5′ by 7′ (it needn't tuck under the pillow). This size can still be used as a wall hanging (anything longer will be difficult to hang). Quilts shown approximately this size are Hattie's, the Artists', and Gini's (Chapters 7, 8, and 11).

MATTRESS TOP MEASUREMENTS

Bed Type	Mattress Size (inches)	Quilt Size	Over Pillow
Crib	28 × 52	44 × 56	44 × 64
Twin	38 × 75	62 × 84	62 × 96
Double	54 × 75	78 × 84	78 × 96
Queen	60 × 75	84 × 84	84 × 96
King	72 × 75 or 85	96 × 96	96 × 106
Water bed	72 × 104	80 × 118	80 × 127

QUILT MOTHER'S CHECKLIST

1. OCCASION _____

Ideas: Wedding, anniversary, birthday, centennial, retirement, birth, award ceremony, raffle, friendship, exhibition, commemorative, class (see Chapter 2)

2. GROUP _____

Ideas: Family, relatives, neighbors, church group, quilting group, school classes, wedding shower guests, club groups, special interest group, community members, church members, sewing organizations, friends

3. QUILT DESIGNER(S) _____

Ideas: You, mother of the bride, friend who sews, quilting group member, couple of friends, grandmother, teacher, guild committee chairperson, sister, daughter, anybody who is willing and can sew, anybody who is a good organizer and knows people who sew (see individual quilts)

4. ORGANIZATION STYLE _____

Ideas: "Anything goes" squares, provided background square, partially completed background square, kit including square and fabrics, collected signatures, exchange of blocks, assigned designs, quilting group (see Chapter 2)

5. THEME _____

Ideas: Signatures, monograms, sayings, shared memories, common symbols, random patches (crazy quilt), traditional patterns, patriotic imagery, local scenes, flowers, pets, decorations (buttons and bows), drawings, self-portraits, cutout figures, award ribbons, commercial logos, favorite stories, historic scenes, seasons, nursery rhyme characters, and so on (see Chapter 2 and individual quilts)

6. TECHNIQUE _____

Ideas: Hand appliqué, machine appliqué, decorative embroidery, satin stitch embroidery, machine embroidery, free-motion machine stitching, couching, counted cross stitch, pieced blocks, attached objects, photographic images, textile paints, acrylic paints, crayon transfer, felt cutout figures (see Chapters 6 through 10)

7. TIME

Ideas: Allow time to request squares, make kits, make squares, collect squares; aim for date of wedding shower, anniversary, or other special occasion; pick an arbitrary date—don't leave it open-ended

8. QUILT SIZE

Ideas: Single, double, king or queen bed size, coverlet size, baby crib size, wall hanging, table cover, pillow cover (see following section for specific dimensions)

9. BLOCK SIZE AND SHAPE

Ideas: 6- to 16-inch squares, rectangles, strips, irregular patches, cutout figures, random cutout shapes (see Julie's Quilt, Chapter 10)

10. LAYOUT

Ideas: Joined squares, grid with borders, checkerboard, center medallion, random patches, random placement, American flag style (see following section for grid layouts)

11. COLORS

Ideas: Honoree's decorating theme, seasonal theme, full color range, limited range (see Chapter 5 for a discussion of color planning)

12. FABRICS

Ideas: Quilting cottons, elegant novelty fabrics, lightweight wools, assorted plain-weave fabrics (see Chapter 4)

13. YARDAGE

Information on how to compute yardage for a quilt, once you've decided on size and layout, follows later in this chapter

14. QUILTING METHOD

Ideas: All-over quilting stitches, outline quilting stitches, in-the-ditch machine quilting, knotted quilting, button-stitch quilting, Amish quilting (see Chapter 12)

15. DISPLAY

Ideas: Bed, wall hanging, window cover, exhibition, raffle (see Chapter 13)

The largest quilt in this book is Colleen's queen-sized 81" by 96" (see Chapter 12). Strength and skill are required to cope with the volume and weight of the fabrics and filler. Since most friendship quilts are wall-hung these days, consider the smaller sizes.

Figuring Size and Quantity of Blocks

There are several ways to determine the size of squares or blocks: (1) Start with the number of friends in your group to determine the number of blocks, then decide the block size you want and let these two figures determine the quilt size; (2) start with the quilt size, subtract a border amount of about 10" all around, subtract spacers or sashing, and divide the remaining area by the number of squares you need to determine block size; or (3) decide on a standard block size, say 8", 12", or 16", and make the quilt whatever size works out with the number of blocks you will have.

Block sizes on the quilts shown varied from 6" squares for the Minister's Retirement Quilt, to 12" squares for Claudia's, Gini's and Colleen's quilts. The 9½" blocks on Peter's Quilt were probably the easiest for people to decorate—not too big and not too small.

Make the blocks square, unless you begin the design, as on Kim's Quilt. Amy's blocks were 8" × 11" horizontal, and at least one came back vertical. When this happens, you may be able to trim the top and bottom, then piece the sides to make a horizontal block.

Laying Out the Quilt Top

Dimensions and block sizes are given for each quilt in the book, along with layout diagrams or photographs.

On most friendship quilts, sashings of various widths are used between the blocks to separate them and help to hold the design together. You can set the blocks without lattice, as in the Artists' Quilt (Chapter 8), where alternating background colors separate the squares.

Compare the sizes of the quilts and the number of blocks in the layouts to see what suits your group best. Mary's Quilt has the fewest blocks with 12, and the Minister's Retirement Quilt the most with 80. Keep your layout as flexible as possible, since you may have to change it if fewer (or more) blocks come back than you had planned.

Following are some possible layouts—and suggestions for handling uneven numbers of returnees.

12 blocks: 3 across, 4 vertical
13 or 14 blocks: make a pillow from one, or add 1 or 2 blocks
15 blocks: 3 across, 5 vertical
16 blocks: 4 across, 4 vertical; add wider—or additional—top and bottom borders
17 blocks: make a pillow from one
18 blocks: 3 across, 6 vertical; use horizontal blocks
19 blocks: add one block
20 blocks: 4 across, 5 vertical
21 blocks: 3 across, 7 vertical; add side borders
22 or 23 blocks: add two to three blocks to make 24 or 25
24 blocks: 4 across, 6 vertical
25 blocks: 5 across, 5 vertical; add top and bottom borders or keep quilt square
26, 27, 29, 31 blocks: add or subtract blocks for a workable layout; make pillows from "extra" blocks
28 blocks: 4 across, 7 vertical
30 blocks: 5 across, 6 vertical

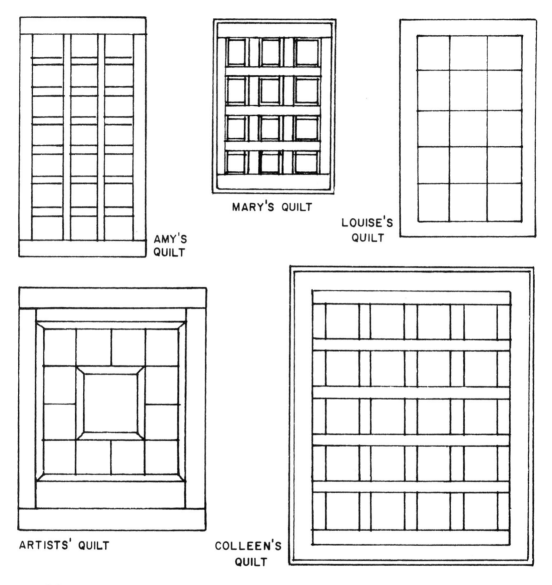

AMY'S QUILT: 44" × 80"; 21 blocks, 8" × 11" rectangles; 2" lattice; 3½" side borders, 5½" top and
    bottom borders.

MARY'S QUILT: 42½" × 58½"; 12 blocks, 8" square; ½" frames, 2¾" lattice; 4½" side borders, 6½"
    top and bottom borders; ½" binding.

LOUISE'S QUILT: 47½" × 72½"; 15 blocks, 12½" square; all 5" borders.

ARTISTS' QUILT: 64" × 79"; 12 blocks, 12½" square, plus center 22" square; 1½" frames; 6¼" strip
    at top, 9¼" strip at bottom; 5¼" border.

COLLEEN'S QUILT: 81" × 96"; 12 blocks, 12" square; 3" lattice; 9" border, ½" binding.

Fig. 3–6 Five successful quilt block arrangements.

Figuring Yardage Widths

Most quilting fabric is 45" wide. The selvage is not usable since it may shrink, so 44" is the width for computing fabric amounts. All fabric amounts in the quilt directions are computed on this width. I'd hoped to include conversion charts for other widths, but the placement would not be the same, so simple area conversion does not work. For example, for a 72"-wide quilt, you will still need twice the length for backing, whether the fabric is 54" or 60" wide—or only 45". It's best to draw your fabric layout on graph paper to determine correct amounts.

If the quilt will be washed, all fabrics should be washed before you send out squares, or lay out or measure borders and sashing.

Wait until you know for certain how many blocks you will be arranging before you cut the borders and sashings. Consult your graph plan before you cut or tear. Place the largest pieces first. Plan to make all long pieces run with the grain (lengthwise). If you need to divide the quilt backing, divide it in the center or add to both sides equally.

Make sure all spacers run in the same direction on the grain, especially with prints. Yardage given for quilts is always based on all border and lattice pieces running lengthwise on 44"-wide fabric unless otherwise specified. Don't plan your layout too tightly in case of mistakes. Buy a little extra fabric, since you'll probably need it.

Graphing a Layout

Laying out the quilt pieces on graph paper allows you to measure yardage accurately and plan a cutting layout. For doing this, you'll need a calculator, a ruler, a pencil (with eraser), and graph paper. I suggest you use graph paper that is eight squares to the inch (the inch marked in a wider blue line). Choose a scale, such as 1" equals 1'. This means that each square on ⅛" graph paper would equal 4½". With this small scale, I was able to get all the yardages on one page in the diagram for Peter's Quilt. On it, 1" = 36", so ¼" equals 9" or ⅛" equals 4½".

A calculator comes in handy for adding a series of measurements, multiplying a series of dimensions, dividing yardage into units, and converting yardage to percentages for easier adding. I've included a conversion chart contributed by my husband Cap.

CONVERSION CHART FOR YARDAGE

Fraction of a Yard	% of a Yard	Inches	Fraction of a Yard	% of a Yard	Inches
⅛	12.5	4½	1⅛	112.5	40½
¼	25.0	9	1¼	125.0	45
⅓	33.3	12	1⅓	133.3	48
⅜	37.5	13½	1⅜	137.5	49½
½	50.0	18	1½	150.0	54
⅝	62.5	22½	1⅝	162.5	58½
⅔	66.7	24	1⅔	166.7	60
¾	75.0	27	1¾	175.0	63
⅞	87.5	31½	1⅞	187.5	67½
1	100.0	36	2	200.0	72

Yardage is always rounded off to the next largest fraction, the standard ones used in measuring yardage. Price charts in fabric stores are keyed to these amounts, as a rule, so it is difficult to buy in-between amounts.

For most quilt pieces, I've added a ½″ seam allowance, but in practice I give border, backing, and block pieces 1″ seam allowances just in case. Since I always mark the quilt pieces with seam lines on the back, these dimensions aren't too critical. I can always trim off the extra. If you don't mark, but sew seams using your sewing machine guide, you'll have to measure and cut most carefully.

Now let's run through the layout diagram of Peter's Quilt to see how to figure one of your own.

Laying Out Peter's Quilt

Peter's Quilt measures 68″ wide and 82″ long. It has 30 blocks, measuring 9½″ square, with 6″ borders and 2″ × 9½″ lattice. The backing, border and lattice are cut from the same dark brown fabric. The background squares are all the same off-white fabric, and five colors of appliqué fabric are provided.

First I drew a diagram to scale on graph paper, measured piece sizes, and kept track of all the pieces needed. I used a pencil for these drawings so I could easily make changes.

Next, I measured and drew an open-ended rectangle 1¼″ wide and about 7″ long to represent the 44″-wide backing and border fabric. The backing pieces are the largest, so I placed them within this diagram first. Since the backing is wider than the fabric, I divided it in half and added seam allowances. As

you can see, I had to lay these pieces end-to-end.

On the quilt face, the side border is the same length as the assembled blocks. Two of these pieces will fit beside the quilt backs on my diagram. The top and bottom borders are the width of the quilt, plus seam allowances. I placed these lengthwise on the diagram.

Next I added ½″ seam allowances to the four vertical spacers, which are the same length as the side borders, and fit them on the diagram. I added ½″ seam allowances to the 30 spacers and clustered them on the diagram, all running in the same lengthwise direction.

All pieces fit within 7″ on the graph; each inch equals one yard, so I needed seven yards of brown print border and backing fabric. For the 30 squares measuring 9½″ plus seam allowance, I calculated off-white fabric totaling 2½ yards.

For the appliqué pieces, I planned to divide one yard of fabric into 32 pieces, placing 8 across, each 5½″ wide, and 4 lengthwise, 9″ long. So I needed one yard each of peach, blue, mauve, green, and gold fabric. The total yardage for Peter's Quilt was figured at 14½ yards (see materials list in the Quilt Profile).

Scheduling Time

We decided to make Peter's Quilt when Mom and Lois visited me in June. We purchased the yardage, made up the kits, and mailed them out within a week. Completed squares came back in September. This allowed plenty of time for me to set the face blocks, assemble the quilt, and even hand-quilt in front of the TV before the December wedding.

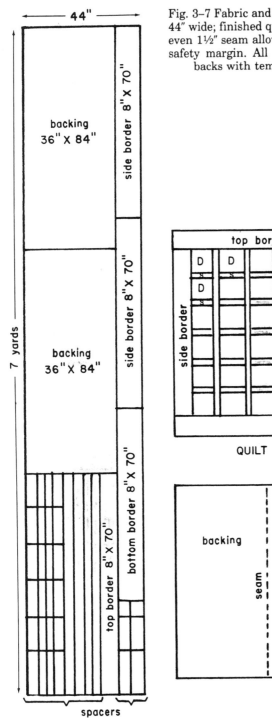

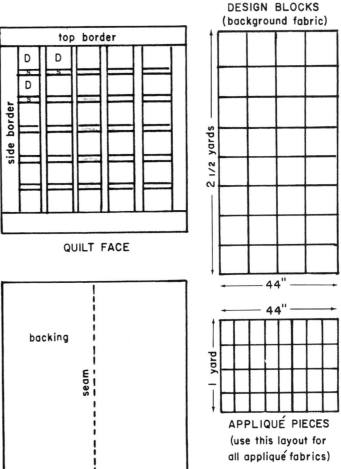

Fig. 3–7 Fabric and layout diagrams for Peter's quilt. All fabrics 44″ wide; finished quilt size is 67½″ × 79″. Note that I add 1″ or even 1½″ seam allowances on borders, blocks, and binding for a safety margin. All actual dimensions *must be marked* on the backs with templates when you vary seam allowances.

Most of the quilts described in this book took from two to six months to complete. Members of the Unitarian Church group stitched 80 blocks at circle meetings and coffee klatches. Their quilt took about six months of sporadic quilting to finish. Julie's Quilt made up the fastest. We all stenciled and textile-painted heart shapes at the shower, and Leslie assembled them into a wall hanging in a matter of days. Louise's antique quilt took the longest, as indicated by the dates embroidered on it stretching from 1892 to 1898.

Several factors help speed up making friendship quilts. Traditionally, they do not need to be as fully quilted as quilts intended for heavy use. Bonded batting requires fewer quilting stitches than loose batting. Machine sewing really speeds the process. These factors, and the event for which the quilt is planned, enforce a deadline.

If you place high requirements on contributed squares (such as 8 solid square inches of hand-embroidered satin-stitching) you will need six months to a year to complete the quilt. More casual contributions needn't take more than two or three months to do.

Don't Count Your Chickens

Wait until all the blocks are returned before you measure and cut the borders and backing. You may need to rearrange your layout plan. Not only that, friends may have added enough unusual embellishments to alter the color scheme and force you to select another, more neutral border fabric.

Fig. 3–8 Strange bedfellows meet on Peter's Quilt, in this case Sandy's aunt and uncle, and Peter's brother Rick going uphill on his motorcycle.

47

Peter's Wedding Quilt

QUILT PROFILE

OCCASION: The Christmas wedding of Peter Goodrich and Sandy Arner in Bethlehem, Pennsylvania.

GROUP: Parents and grandparents of the bride and bridegroom; brothers, cousins, Penn State pals, and assorted relatives and friends.

QUILT DESIGNERS: Sisters Lois Vosburg Goodrich and Carolyn Vosburg Hall.

ORGANIZATION: Friends and relatives were geographically too scattered (New York, Michigan, Florida) for a get-together wedding shower, so kits were mailed to participants in July. Blocks came back in September and the completed quilt was the hit of the rehearsal dinner. It even made a circuit around the wedding reception for all to see and admire.

THEME: Shared memories. There's a group of fellow Penn State supporters saying "Go Lions"; a Bible and cross relating to the Bethlehem wedding location. Brothers and cousins gave advice: "Live Free or Die"; "If life's a roller coaster, enjoy the ride"; and "Let's Go!" Grandmothers made charming scenes of houses, flowers, and fishing in Florida. Lois and I made cats.

TECHNIQUE: Appliquéd designs and scenes on light background blocks in machine appliqué, hemmed and hand-sewn appliqué, basting stitch embroidery.

TIME: 7 months at a leisurely pace

SIZE: 67½" × 79"

BLOCK SIZE: 9½" squares

LAYOUT: 30 blocks, 5 squares horizontally, 6 squares vertically; 6" border; 2" lattice

COLORS: Off-white background squares; designs in peach, gold print, blue print, green print, and mauve print; border and lattice in dark brown print

FABRICS: Quilting cottons

YARDAGE TOTAL: 14½ yards

FILLER: Bonded poly-fiberfill quilt batting

QUILTING METHOD: Comforter style, hand-quilted around the squares

DISPLAY: Sandy and Peter mounted the quilt on the wall in their handsome big-city apartment as the focal point of the living room

MATERIALS

(Buy extra fabric for safety margin)

Design blocks: thirty 9½" squares, plus 1½" seam allowances, off-white firmly woven background fabric, sturdy enough for machine appliqué	2½ yards
Borders, sashing, backing: dark brown print	7 yards
Border: two pieces, 8" × 69", vertical; two pieces 8" × 68½", horizontal	
Sashing: four pieces, 3" × 70"	
Backing: two pieces, 35¾" × 81"	
Appliqué fabrics: one yard each plain peach, dusty sky blue, dusty light green, mauve, light gold print, cut into 5½" × 9" pieces	5 yards
Total	14½ yards

Filler: bonded quilting batt, 68" × 82"

Other supplies: sewing threads in assorted colors for seams and appliqué; glue and baste sticks; sharp scissors; sewing machine needles; hand needles; seam ripper; template cardboard

PROCEDURE

1. Assemble fabrics and supplies. Cut out pattern pieces.

2. Assemble the kits to include one off-white background square and five colored squares, each 5½" × 9". Include instructions on the invitation for making the square.

3. Collect the blocks. Finish or repair any squares that need help. For example, take out puckered machine stitching, back with stabilizer and resew with matching thread, or darker thread for outline emphasis. (Most people can't tell you redid their square. They decide something in the quilting process makes it look better.)

4. For complete information on assembling the quilt face and quilting the layers, see Chapters 11 and 12.

Chapter 4

Ways to Include Friends

Kim's Valentine Quilt

When we made Claudia's Wedding Quilt, we knew all of her friends would enjoy the challenge of making a quilt block, but what about people we didn't know? How would Kim's friends feel about opening a shower invitation to find a fabric square to complete? Pleasure? Horror?

The goal of a friendship quilt is to include friends, not to terrify them with demands. Even so, the quilt designer does need to be specific in some requirements, or the quilt turns out to be a waste of fabric and will be hidden away. What's the solution to this problem?

Providing Partly Completed Squares

For Kim, we tried something new. Kim is Rosemary's daughter and she received the second quilt organized by the Rosemary–Leslie–Helen–Carolyn team, since she was the next of the group's daughters to become engaged. We decided to partly finish each block, so that no one would be intimidated. As you can see by the delightful finished quilt, this was a successful approach when we had no way to assess sewing skills of contributors.

I chose a range of fabric colors Kim liked, avoiding red—a distinct dislike. Since it was near Valentine's Day, I cut out 5″ × 6″ hearts in hot pink, dusty pink, soft purple, and American Beauty rose red (you've gotta' have red on a Valentine quilt; this muted red served as the dark color rather than the bright).

A heart shape in one of the four colors was machine appliquéd to the center of a background block (accurately placed to give a repetitive overall pattern). Friends were requested to embellish the heart with little or lots of embroidery, lace, buttons, or bows. The only requirement was to include their signature. Anyone who wished could return the block for me to sew for her.

All Kim's friends seemed delighted to be a part of the finished quilt. And, of course, we all ooh'd and ahh'd with genuine pleasure as each block was revealed.

Just to make sure all goes well, keep the following points in mind while planning your quilt and composing the invitation to request blocks.

The Invitation to Participate

Discover what the group of block makers can handle in terms of skills,

50

Fig. 4–1 Kim Squires' February wedding shower prompted a Valentine theme, with hearts in pink, deep red, and lavender on white.

Fig. 4–2 Kim's mother Rosemary used fabric from the bride's and bridesmaids' dresses. I used lace, the names, and the date of the shower.

time, and confidence. You'll always be surprised at the exquisite quality of some blocks, and the devil-may-care look of others, but expect this diversity. Blocks won't all look as if done by the same hand. If you want a more consistent type of quilt, make Hattie's pieced-block quilt where requirements are tight and the variation is limited to signatures.

Don't ask too much or it may be hard to get people to participate. Expert quilters might be happy and willing to make a complex block if the honoree is a close friend, if the block maker gets a block in return, or if it's for a worthy cause, such as community spirit or world peace.

Choose a type of organization suited to the group. Whenever possible, it's fun to get together to compare blocks, exchange ideas, and chat in the same way the quilting bee has functioned for ages. Women too busy and too energetic to sit idle-handed enjoy this kind of meeting. Community quilts, church quilts and quilting group quilts are made this way. It can work even at a single meeting, such as a wedding shower, if the time is devoted solely to this task, and uncomplicated results are requested.

For the most control over color and texture, provide fabric background squares and appliqué swatches, embroidery flosses, or whatever is needed for the chosen technique. Not everyone will have supplies on hand or access to them. Most quilts benefit from this consistency, but if your group is a bunch of individualists who want to design unhampered, like Elaine Morse's Unitarians, you may prefer to make an anything-goes quilt, like the one in Chapter 2.

Instructions to Contributors

Provide complete but brief directions on what you expect. More than one page of instructions will most likely go unread. Specify such points as what technique to use, what theme, how much seam allowance, how and where to sign (and stitch) names, and whether washability is important. Let participants know whether or not they can add other fabrics, different colors, or miscellaneous trims. Include the deadline, and tell people what to do if they can't meet it. If you're willing, include an offer of assistance for people who want help.

Make the tone of the invitation friendly and enthusiastic so people will want to participate. And be gracious to those who decline. Include your phone number and address so participants can ask questions, and know where to return their squares.

Make sure information appears in a useful, clear order. You want to be friendly, but not wordy, and make it sound like fun to participate.

A sample of Kim's invitation is shown in Figure 4–3 with instructions for making a quilt like hers. Figure 4–4 shows a sample invitation that you might use for a quilt like Kim's if you want to have more control over the squares returned than if you use an invitation like the one in Figure 4–3. If you want to photocopy it — or any other invitation — for your own use, lay opaque white paper over the parts you don't want. Then you can fill in the blanks by hand or typewriter. A quicker way is to type or write your own words on opaque white paper the size to cover unwanted words in the invitation, and paste patches in place on the invitation. Photocopy the invitations, enhance them with color if desired, and send them out.

Photocopying is convenient, inexpensive, and will save having to write 20 or more invitations. This also allows you to embellish the directions with quilt designs, details of embroidery stitches, or other drawings. Add some color to the finished copies with colored pencils, markers, water colors or stickers.

What If You Are Asked to Make a Quilt Block?

Now for the other side of the coin: You've opened the mail and there is a square to complete. What now? First read the directions carefully; if they are specific, then follow the theme suggested and the technique requested. Stick to the color scheme if one is specified. People really care about color, and unusual additions will be difficult to integrate into the quilt. The tone of the invitation will give a good idea of what the quilt designer expects. If it's breezy and open, encouraging you to use any color, add any trim, and doesn't say "washable," then no holds are barred. Make any kooky, wonderful block that comes to mind.

Don't worry about your design or sewing skills. You were invited because they want you to be included, not because you won a prize for sewing. Accept the challenge. So what if the quilt designer is an expert? It's not a contest but a collaboration. Ask for help if you need it, but give it a try. You might surprise yourself. You can borrow ideas from any number of places, and get help from friends or from the quilt designer.

Come join in making
a friendship quilt
for _____ to celebrate _____
Enclosed is a quilt square with an
appliqued heart for you to embellish
as you wish.
Add embroidery and other washable
trims: lace, ribbons & beads in
related colors.
Embroider your name or have a friend
do it for you.
If you don't have time, send me your
square, along with your design ideas,
and I will sew it for you.

Bring or send the finished
square to me by _____
Thanks for joining in
this keepsake quilt.

_____
_____
_____

Fig. 4–3 Kim's Valentine Quilt invitation. The contributor can also use the heart as a pattern for the quilt block.

To the Friends of *Kim* *and* *Louis*

You are invited to join in making a friendship group quilt for *Kim* to celebrate her marriage to *Louis* on *date* . This is a chance to share in a very special hand-made gift.

Enclosed are a washed and ironed background fabric block and *appliqué fabrics* in *Kim's* colors. Please design something on your square that will remind her of you, and don't forget to sign your name as part of the finished quilt block. Plan your design to fit within a 9½" square, leaving 1" seam allowances so I can set the blocks together.

To make your design, use this technique. Cut out and appliqué your design to the background square. If you machine appliqué, pin the square to preshrunk white lining fabric or removable backing paper to stabilize the background fabric, or use a hoop to avoid puckering while you sew. A fabric glue stick is handy to hold the pieces in place.

Add embroidery and other washable trims such as beads, ribbon, and lace in this color range if you wish.

Embroidering your name can be the hardest part. If you would like me to machine embroider it for you, sign your name in letters ½" high on a slip of paper and pin it in place. Please write, since a continuous line is easier for me to stitch.

P.S. If you haven't time or hate to sew, return your fabric block and fabrics, along with your design idea, and I'll complete it for you.

S.O.S. If you need help or ruin your square, I have extra fabric. Call me at _____ or write to me at _____ .

Bring your finished block to the shower so blocks can all be displayed; the quilt will then be completed by the wedding date.

Thanks for joining in the quilt. It will be a keepsake.

(Signature)

Fig. 4–4 A sample of more elaborate instructions for a quilt similar to Kim's. Replace *italic* words with your own specifics.

If you can't complete the block for any reason, call or write the quilt designer and return the block with your apologies. The quilt designer expects this may happen with a few people, and she'll probably offer to help you make it or do it for you. Every quilt designer I've talked with said she does an average of three to five blocks per quilt for people and enjoys doing them. So do I. None of us wants people to be left out because of limited sewing skills or other problems.

Meet the deadline. Just like a bridge game, or a doubles tennis match, the quilt can't proceed until all the participants are there. Let the quilt designer know if you are going to be late. There's probably some leeway in the time schedule for this possibility.

You may discover when you see the finished quilt that the designer has strengthened some of your stitching or resewn parts to smooth out puckers. Don't be offended. In the process of making the quilt, and in years to come, there's a lot of stress on the stitching. The stronger it is, the longer it will last. On the other hand, no one should alter your block substantially without consulting you first.

Sources of Ideas for Imagery

Two factors in particular will influence the scenes, sayings, or designs you will choose to put on the quilt block.

1. The theme will suggest ideas, as it is meant to. As you've noticed throughout this book, some images are quite common and appropriate: people's houses, gardens, and pets; slo-gans ("Go, Lions, Go," and "If mother says no, ask grandmother," from Peter's Quilt); and common symbols, such as hearts, flowers, birthday cakes, wedding rings, and traditional quilt patterns.

2. If the invitation asks for a certain technique, this will suggest designs and ways of making them. For example, most appliqué designs are fairly simple since complex ones with tiny parts are hard to make in fabric. Cross stitch designs must be planned on a grid. Pieced blocks must follow a certain geometric simplicity to look right.

Within the limitations of theme and technique, almost anything is possible. Peter's Quilt has a roller coaster and a motorcycle on it. The Minister's has the airline symbol for Sarasota; Claudia's has a camera. People chose these as representative of their shared interests with the honoree. What comes to your mind—a certain car, a remarkable hat, a favorite store, a funny incident? Look through photograph albums for scenes, people, characteristic dress, and poses.

Dover publishes a wide assortment of books with all kinds of designs to copy or trace. These include designs from many eras and cultures (Victorian, Greek, American Indian, Art Nouveau, Art Deco), monograms, animals, symbols, and more. These books may be available at your library. If not, other books with good ideas will abound there. Look in the art section, at Quarto books (oversized books), natural history books, and children's books, all places where there will be many fine photographs and illustrations. Catalogs are another source of ideas.

Fit the Imagery
to the Technique

Once you've found the idea you want, fit it to a suitable technique. Study the examples shown in various technique chapters to see which designs work best. Pieced patchwork blocks never have squiggly lines, cross stitch has tiny detail, appliqué commonly has large solid areas of color, and embroidery does not. Keep this in mind while you choose and adapt your imagery. The designs that look best are those which are best suited to the way they are made.

Working from Photos
and Drawings

To make an appliqué block from a photo or drawing, use an illustration that is the right size or use an opaque projector (kid's toy or artist's tool) to project it full size, and trace it. Lacking this, you can draw a grid on tracing paper, trace the image and enlarge it by making a bigger grid and tracing the lines. Or ask a local photocopy center to photocopy or photostat the image to the size you want.

Simplifying Designs

For the cat on Peter's Quilt, I found a photo of a cat just the right size, and put it on the light box to trace. You can use a window or a glass-topped table for tracing, too. In the photograph I could see a million individual fur strands, but I planned to appliqué it, not embroider every strand. I needed to simplify.

There are several ways to do this. One of the easiest is to squint at the

Fig. 4–5 The pattern for this machine-appliquéd cat was drawn by tracing over a photograph, simplifying shading and color demarcation.

photo. This way you won't see detail but light and dark areas. Laying tracing paper over the photo will also mute the detail so you can simplify. Trace the large areas, indicating which are light and which dark. Add enough detail (eyes, nose) so the cat is recognizable.

Using an opaque projector helps you to simplify. If you project an image and trace it, you'll automatically select a limited number of lines to trace, rather than put in every hair. Mark lines where colors meet, where shadows and highlights meet. This tracing paper drawing can be used as a pattern for cutting pieces and a stitching guide for appliqué.

If the photograph shows an odd angle, as a house might, don't use the tracing as is. Claudia's house on Pe-ter's Quilt is not a literal copy. She straightened lines from the photograph and accentuated the high points. She made the doors and windows bigger. Children do this kind of selective simplification automatically.

Fig. 4–6 Jean Schuler satin-stitched simple stick figures; Mary Toot's musical notes provide a distinctive autograph; Claudia Stroud hand-stitched her "country" heart; Janet Jung adorned hers with rows of rickrack.

Disneyland uses it well, too, making three-quarter-scale houses with full-sized doors and windows, and you don't even notice. It just feels right.

Jean Schuler's stick figures on Kim's Valentine Quilt (Fig. 4–6) are close to the ultimate in simplification. These line drawings work well because the embellishments on the hearts are mostly embroidered and linear. Linear people fit with linear embroideries. The imagery fits the technique.

Following Your Instincts

If you find an idea forming in your mind, but you think it might not fit in, it will look dreadful, people will laugh, or it will never turn out and you can't do it, don't be intimidated by this attack of Artist's Anxieties. No matter how good you become as an artist, you will still have some of that worry. That's not bad, though. You can use this anxiety as artists do. It spurs you on to do the best you can, like stage fright.

It may be comforting to know that many of the people making squares for the quilt have the same concerns as you. Most friendship quilts are made by amateurs, by people's friends. Trust your instincts. After all, it's your friend who asked you to be on the quilt. Do what you feel pleasure in doing. The feelings you put into your work will show.

Some of the suggestions I've made in this book will certainly get me banned from the purist quilters' society (mixing hand and machine sewing willy-nilly, quilting every 12" instead of every 2", for example) but these shortcuts and easier techniques allow everyone to participate. The point is that we are all going to be on that friendship quilt together.

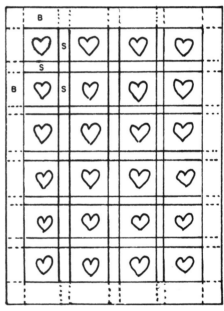

B : 5 1/2" border
S : 2 1/4" lattice
♡ : 9 1/2" design blocks

Fig. 4–7 Diagram of Kim's quilt, 55¾" × 77½".

Kim's Valentine Quilt

QUILT PROFILE

OCCASION: Kim Squires planned to marry Louis Kunimatsu; a February wedding shower was planned for presenting the quilt blocks.

GROUP: Friends and relatives

QUILT DESIGNER: Carolyn Vosburg Hall

ORGANIZATION: Partially completed blocks, small fabric swatches, and suggestions for trimming the appliquéd designs were sent to contributors to embellish as they chose.

THEME: Decorated hearts in romantic colors for Valentine's Day, with signatures.

TECHNIQUE: Machine-appliquéd hearts on background blocks were decorated by friends in many ways: by hand and machine appliqué, by hand and machine embroidery, by borders of lace, eyelet, and rickrack, and added buttons, ribbons and bows. Kim's mother, Rosemary, added some lace and net from Kim's wedding veil, Leslie added candy-sweet colors of fabric in strips, Claudia made her heart into a Pennsylvania Dutch style flower, Mary Toot made musical notes (a pun), Jean Schuler made stick figures and Gloria Dittmers stuffed her heart, trapunto-style. We were impressed with the variety. I stitched the date of the shower and the names of the bride and bridegroom.

TIME: Invitations went out in January for the February 11 shower, and the quilt was completed before the spring wedding.

SIZE: 53¾" by 77½"

BLOCK SIZE: 9½" squares

BLOCK AND LAYOUT: 24 blocks, 4 across, 6 high; 2¼" lattice, 5½" border

FABRIC & YARDAGE TOTAL: 10 yards of quilting cottons, print Indian Head-style decorating cotton

FILLER: bonded polyester quilt batt

COLORS: Off-white poly cotton background blocks; hearts in deep rose red, hot pink, dusty pink, and periwinkle purple; appliqué swatches in each of the four colors, plus a cream-and-pink print; deep periwinkle purple polka dot for the border.

QUILTING METHOD: Comforter style, hand-quilted around blocks

DISPLAY: Kim and Louis decorated their bedroom to match the quilt. Kim and Rosemary used the extra fabric (I always buy more than required) for curtain borders and tiebacks, and painted the walls to harmonize.

MATERIALS

(Buy extra fabric for safety margin)

Design blocks: twenty-four 10½″ squares (including seam allowance), off-white poly/cotton firmly woven fabric	1¾ yards
Borders and backing: purple print fabric	6⅛ yards
Lattice: five 3″ × 49″ strips; eighteen 3″ × 10″ pieces	
Border: two 6½″ × 67½″ side strips; two 6½″ × 56¾″ top and bottom strips	
Backing: 56¾″ × 78½″	
Appliqué fabrics: ⅞ yard each of five colors—pink, purple print, dusty rose, deep red, cream and pink print; each color cut into twenty-eight pieces 7″ × 9″	4 yards
Total	11⅞ yards

Filler: bonded polyester quilting batt, 56″ × 78″
Other supplies: assorted machine sewing and hand embroidery threads in harmonizing colors; sewing machine; safety pins; 2″ quilting pins; 24″ quilting hoop

PROCEDURE

1. Assemble the fabrics and supplies, and cut out the listed pieces (all pieces have ½″ seam allowances).

2. Request the blocks. In this case, not knowing the sewing skills of the couple's friends, we sent pre-appliquéd heart blocks (and tried to match one of the four heart colors to the friend's color preferences). When the blocks were completed, Kim and her mother preferred a different border color than originally chosen. We found the beautiful purple print seen on the quilt.

3. Assemble the quilt face (see Chapter 11) and then assemble and quilt the layers according to directions in Chapter 12.

Chapter 5

Choosing Colors

Lori's Wedding Quilt

Lori hates green. This is not a passing fancy. As an artist, she thinks about color a great deal, and green doesn't sing to her soul. Well, maybe a bright acid green—like a Granny Smith apple—does: but most greens, no.

Lori was my first apprentice. Her mom's a potter and her dad a painter, so she understood that art is more work than wishing. When she wanted to learn about fiber arts, she came to work with me. When she married, I was eager to make her a friendship quilt. "Remember that she hates green," her mom said.

Even though I went to the fabric store alone this time, Lori was with me as "we" chose purples, pinks, blacks, and muted blues—colors nobody could put green with. But they did! And I must admit that I used a militant hand to tame those colors that didn't work on this quilt.

Everyone has an inherent color sense—Lori, her friends who picked green, and me. We all know what we like, what we don't, even if we can't say why. Artists may well have a more acute color sense because they deal with color all the time and perceive colors so intensely. Discovering all the nuances of color is a lifetime process. If you are reading this book, you most likely have an active color sense, and can develop it even more. Learning about color helps you to trust your own color sense.

Color Sense: Everybody's Got One

Once long ago I had a periwinkle purple wall in one of the kid's bedrooms. I'd go in and inhale that wonderful color. Eventually I painted it a certain blue to match a color in new curtains, and couldn't stand it! Three weeks of rushing past it, and I had to repaint that heavy color. (I now hated the curtains and got rid of them, too.). This whole episode astonished me. How could a simple color do that? Normally I'd be too frugal, too busy, and perhaps too unwilling to admit I made a mistake to change a new wall color, but my color sense demanded that I get rid of a color I couldn't abide.

Many factors help to form one's sense of color. First, personality dictates color preferences. Colors project emotions. Certainly you know "red" people who are lively and energetic, or have met a "yellow" person who is sunny natured and optimistic. And

Fig. 5–1 Friends who contributed to Lori's Wedding Quilt included artists and grand-mothers. Lori's dad, Russell Bolt, made the "Smile" block; the fish, originally on green fabric, were appliquéd onto a new ground fabric to maintain color scheme. Note that few contributors allowed the unbleached muslin background to show on their blocks.

how about the "blue" person who is gentle, loyal and subdued? People who prefer white are said to be positive and pure. Those who like "brown" are earthy and sensitive.

Most of us have bits and pieces of many moods at different times; each different shade of a color projects a slightly different mood; combinations of colors have more complex effects: so don't take color "labels" too literally. However, the group of colors you choose for a quilt creates its "personality." You can choose quilt colors in seasonal tones, in colors that look good to eat, or colors that make someone feel cozy, cheerful, or serious.

Color is the most important choice you will make for a quilt. Its size makes it a major focus and a constant influence in a room. Instinctively you make your quilts as beautiful as possible to give everyone pleasure.

In the old days, picking colors was probably easier. Before the nineteenth century, only a limited number of fabric dyes were known, and some were so expensive that only royalty could afford them. Now quilters must make their choices from a bewildering array of plain and printed fabrics in an endless range of color and weave. How does one choose the right colors for a quilt?

The Color Effect of a Quilt

Here are some of the questions to consider when determining a color scheme. The more you know about the honoree, the easier choices will be.

Purpose: Who is it for?
Function: How will it be used?

Effect: What mood are you aiming for?
Consistency: Do the colors suit the design?
Fabrics: What's available?
Style: What does it go with?

Purpose

For a baby's friendship blanket, soft light colors are best so they don't overwhelm the baby's delicate coloring. Older children prefer bright, cheerful colors. If the quilt is for a new bride, ask what color range she is choosing for her home. Amy's Quilt (Chapter 9) has the soft pastels she requested, with touches of brighter colored floss. And we all remember how Lori feels about green.

Function

I often choose the colors needed to fit my idea. The quilt will probably look fine somewhere, but that's not my main concern. I want the colors to express concepts and feelings, and increase the power of the design. The Artists' Quilt is an example of this: I tried fifteen different fabrics before I found the Malaysian batik in brown and purple that could hold its own with the squares.

For Peter's Wedding Quilt, we chose colors for specific imagery—peach for faces and green for grass, for example. This was a successful batch of colors because they complemented each other, had enough contrast with the off-white background, and included a range from light to dark.

Curiously, nobody who sewed a square for Peter's Quilt made their people peach-colored. There are red, green, blue, and gold people, but none peach. Now that I think about it, everyone was probably instinctively choosing personality colors, rather than pictorial colors. I must have picked red for my dad, pictured fishing, to show his vibrant personality.

Mood

Colors create mood. A quilt glowing in soft pastels creates a romantic, feminine effect. The Laura Ashley prints in soft blues, muted greens, and pastel pinks are a good example of this. Amish quilts make a bold statement, sombered by the dark blue or black colors that accompany the solid tones of purple, pink, orange, fuschia, red, green, or blue. If you know what mood you want to achieve, you can select colors that give that effect—for example, bright and bold for a modern quilt, frosty colors for a cool look, or pastels for a dreamy look.

Many old quilts that now have muted tones softly blending together may have been a riot of bright colors when newly constructed and before many washings and beddings. To accomplish this antiqued effect, it is possible to match those faded old colors with new fabrics in muted tones, or even to wash new fabrics in gentle bleach or color remover. Or it may be possible to find old clothing at flea markets to make an "aged quilt." It's the quality and character of the muted colors that gives the antique look.

Consistency

Do the colors you've chosen complement the quilt design? What colors does the design of the quilt suggest? Hattie's Birthday Quilt in pieced blocks is traditional in style; it's hard to imagine making this quilt in bright red, yellow, and blue.

If the person who will receive the quilt has suggested a color range, this probably tells you what kind of design that person likes, such as bright colors for bold modern or muted colors for country. Relate the colors and the design as much as possible.

Fabrics

To a certain extent, you are limited in color to what the fabric stores have in stock. There are seasonal changes when some colors or fabrics are hard to find; for this reason, when I see a fabric I love or need, I buy a yard or more. Sometimes the border color you have chosen does not go with the completed squares, or the recipient doesn't like it. This means a trip to the fabric store for a better combination. This happened on more than one quilt included here.

Into storage goes the "wrong" color, because it will be right for something. Yes, I have cupboards full of fabrics. At a sewing conference recently, I saw a coffee mug saying, "The One Who Has the Most Fabrics When She Dies Wins." I knew I was not alone.

Style

Where you live and who you are affect the colors you like. If you drive through the Pennsylvania Dutch countryside to buy a quilt these days, you'll find the colors growing a bit brighter to reflect the tourists' preferences. In Mexico, you'll see rainbows of brilliant colors to match the hot sun. The British tend to like the colorful, flowery look. People who live in cold Northern climates often prefer subdued colors. Victorian homes had somber dark

Fig. 5–2 Lori's mother added textile-marker wording to her block done by machine appliqué (upper left), then added ribbons and trim.

blues and maroons, with dark ornate woods. Ancient Greeks made characteristic black and terra cotta scenes on buff-colored pots. These recognizable tastes from various areas and times create style.

Testing Colors Together

There's no better way to choose colors than by trying them together. No color exists all by itself. Put the blue next to the brown, both next to the pink, and see how they look. It may take hours to make the final choice, but by trial and error you will know what you like and what you don't. Ask a friend with a good "eye" for color if you'd like help. Try some of the following ideas to help choose colors:

1. Study the decorating, style, and home magazines. There's always a major trend in colors—almost yearly in clothing, with a longer cycle for decorating (after all, you've got to keep that couch for more than a year). For other rich and imaginative color schemes, try the art, natural history, and antique magazines and books. If possible, tear out pages and color schemes you like and keep a file or a photo album full of ideas.

2. Don't miss the obvious in the world around you. Study your garden, the fields and roadsides, store windows, clouds and sunsets, buildings. Anything in the landscape may give you a good idea for color combinations. You can't imagine how many greens there are until you walk through a garden or a fruit and vegetable market.

3. Make a collection of colors for testing. It's hard to remember the exact tone of a color and how it relates to another. Collect a supply of paint color chips from the paint store, clip pages of colors from any kind of magazine, make your own color chips by painting colors on squares of paper, buy a sample kit of quality colored papers from the art store, and/or make a collection of small fabric swatches in all colors.

4. Take a tip from artists and keep a sketch book or note pad of color combinations you like. Prismacolor colored pencils are good for notation and graph coloring (see Chapter 7 for detail).

5. Draw your quilt design on graph paper so you know the placement and proportion of the colors. Try lots of color schemes by getting ten or twenty photocopies of this design, then color or paint the designs in various combinations of colors to achieve the effect you want and test your color scheme.

6. Try the colors together in the fabric store. Colors in fabrics look different than colors on paper. When you test fabric bolts together, try to put them in proper proportion. Spread out the background color. Put the border color around it. Try the various other colors with these two and with each other. Yes, it *will* take quite a while, but it's worth it. Don't settle for a color that's almost right, since it will forever be almost right, never perfect.

Color Theory

There are some tried-and-true color concepts: One of the most practical is to begin with a light, a bright, and a dark color. Add muted middle-range colors.

Here's how color theory works. The color wheel was developed on scientific principles. The three primary colors— red, yellow, and blue— cannot be made from other colors. They are the purest, most basic colors of all. If you choose only the three primary colors for a quilt, the effect is like inviting the three most exuberant people you know to a party. It's wild. You don't know where to focus your attention. They all vie for your eyes at once.

Three secondary colors—orange, green, and purple—are made of equal parts of two primaries. These, too, are decisive colors that demand attention.

If you really want a jazzy combination, choose a primary and the secondary color opposite it, called the *complement* and made from the two other primaries. Placing these complementary colors adjacent creates an optical effect that wavers where they meet, a phenomenon Op Art exploited to good advantage.

Primary and secondary colors are all bright, clear colors. They appear on that old famous color wheel, but if you plan to use light, pastel, dark, or grayed colors, where do they come from? Each of the bright, pure colors on the color wheel is called a hue: red,

Fig. 5–3 It takes an artist like Pat Custer Denison, who does stitchery and ceramic tile art, to blend a variety of techniques, fabrics, colors and trim successfully.

blue, orange, green, yellow, and violet. Each hue can vary in value — lighter or darker — and it can vary in intensity — brighter or duller.

Suppose you laid out all the red color swatches you own: I'd like you to meet the Red Hue family. The clearest, brightest red is the most intense version. Those softer shades (rose, russet, mauve and others) are muted, as if the red were mixed with its complement, green. The pink shades are lighter in value, as if white had been added. The maroons are darker in value, as if black had been added.

Now lay out all the greens. You'll see the same wonderful range of colors from bright to muted, and from light to dark. You might think a quilt made from only one color or hue would be dull, but now you can see it could contain a hundred different shades.

Color theory has developed some useful terminology to describe various color combinations. The name for the collection of reds you spread out is *monochrome*, meaning *one color*. The following color schemes give other terms.

Color Schemes

1. *Monochrome* is a single color scheme. Each hue family provides a vast assortment of colors in one hue, like the red group mentioned above.

2. *Analogous colors* are those next to each other on the color wheel. Like cousins, they share some of the same base. Yellow, orange, and red are related. Blue, blue-green and green are analogous. Try applying the light-bright-and-dark system. Choose a light blue-green, a medium green, and a

dark blue, so they don't all vie equally for attention.

3. *Complements* are those shouting opposites mentioned above, but you can calm them down. Starting with red and green, add a dark green, a deep maroon, and a greyed white. If you add a print using combinations of these colors, the red and green are pulled together even better. Hattie's quilt is this type.

4. *Greyed colors* are muted. Color is emotion, and not many of us can stand to live at the top of our emotions all the time. Muted emotions and muted colors are more restful. It's useful to remember that muted colors are toned down by mixing with the complement, or opposite color: This makes for richer, subtler colors. Any of the color schemes — monochromatic, analogous, or light-bright-dark — can work well muted. The strength of Country style is its muted colors.

No matter how many color schemes I suggest, nothing compares with trying colors together. Fabric colors will be different from paint chips, and fabric colors will change in different light. Keep trying colors until you get a good combination and then ask yourself that list of questions: What mood does it project? What should it go with? Who is it for? But the final choice is your eye.

Because quilts are usually made of squares contributed by others, you can't always control what friends will do and this may give your quilt color problems. When a square comes in totally wrong because someone gave it to her aunt to make without mentioning the color limitations, I try to aim for a delicate balance by weighing how the quilt will look against how angry or hurt the square maker might be. Accept this as a challenge of your tact and color sense to make it work.

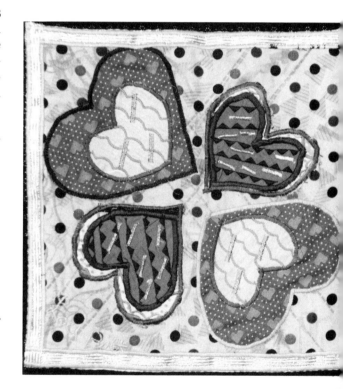

Fig. 5–4 The honoree was invited to make a block for her own quilt. Lori's machine-appliquéd block has multicolored satin stitches and a silver ribbon frame.

Lori's Wedding Quilt

QUILT PROFILE

OCCASION: Lori Bolt,my one-time apprentice and a gifted artist, was marrying sculptor Frank Hassled.

GROUP: Friends, family, relatives, wedding guests

QUILT DESIGNER: Carolyn Vosburg Hall

ORGANIZATION: Geographical distances required sending kits and instructions by mail and return of blocks by mail.

THEME: Signed memories and "personality" squares

TECHNIQUE: Blocks include appliqué by hand and machine, pieced blocks, machine and hand embroidery, and a photo-transfer technique. Ceramic artist Pat Denison picked her own wild colors to make a frizzy-haired lady dancing (Fig. 5–3). Meridith Krell's cactus and purple pie with cherry are wonderfully cryptic (see Fig. 5–1). Lori made a delightful machine-embroidered square for her own quilt (Fig. 5–4). Others added wooden beads, three-dimensional fabric flowers, buttons, lace, and embroidery patches. A painter friend's block grew too thick with paint to send.

TIME: Kits were sent out in June 1985. Squares returned by August 31 were pinned to the border fabric and displayed at Lori and Frank's outdoor wedding (to encourage late square-makers to finish theirs). I completed the quilt in the fall.

SIZE: 53″ × 65″

BLOCKS AND LAYOUT: Twenty 9″-square blocks; 4 across, 5 high; 3″ lattice, 4″ border

COLORS: Appliqué fabrics are light purple, dusty pink print, dusty blue print with pink hearts, maroon print, dusty peach pin dot, and black print. Border is black print and the backing is multicolor print-stripe

FABRIC: Unbleached muslin, quilting cottons

YARDAGE TOTAL: 11¾ yards

BACKING/FILLER: Quilted cotton print (batting included)

QUILTING METHOD: Comforter style, quilt face hand-quilted to the quilted backing

DISPLAY: Lori sewed 2″-wide Velcro to the top back so it could easily be hung in an invitational quilt show of her works and influences. Its companion Velcro strip was stapled up, and the quilt attached.

MATERIALS

(Buy extra fabric for safety margin)

Background squares: medium to heavy unbleached muslin; twenty 9½" blocks	1⅜ yards
Borders and lattices: black print fabric	1⅝ yards
Side borders: 2 strips, 4" × 58"	
Top and bottom borders: 2 strips, 4" × 55"	
Lattice: 31 pieces, 4" × 10"	
Appliqué fabrics: ¾ yard each pink, blue, purple, peach, black, maroon; cut 20 pieces of each color, 9" × 5"	4½ yards
Intersections: sixteen 4" squares of maroon	¼ yard
Backing/filler combo: 54" × 67" quilted backing	4 yards
Total	11¾ yards

Other supplies: assorted harmonizing colors of machine sewing and hand embroidery threads; sewing machine; safety pins, 2" quilting pins; 24" quilting hoop; scissors, hand needles, seam ripper.

PROCEDURE

1. Assemble the fabrics and supplies, and cut out all pieces, which include ½" seam allowances.

2. Some of the changes made on returned blocks for Lori's Wedding Quilt included the following: (1) The unbleached muslin background fabric was too lightweight for machine embroidery (although it could be sewn with stabilizers), and so similar to quilt lining that people covered it all. (2) Squares not large enough were increased in area with added borders. (3) Squares with bright red and bright yellow patches were covered with pink lace to mute the colors. (4) On a green print fabric square sent for me to complete, I cut out the fish and appliquéd them to the quilt colors, then stitched the friend's name by machine.

3. Assemble the quilt face (see Chapter 11).

4. Assemble the layers and complete the quilt as described in Chapter 12.

Chapter 6

Fabrics Plain and Fancy

Louise's Antique Crazy Quilt

Belle Alling Reddin stitched her maiden name in gold-colored silk threads on a swatch of light gray grosgrain ribbon, and then added her married name and the date—June 2, 1892—in silver silk thread. Now that she was the wife of Charles S. Reddin, a bank architect, and living in a lovely mansion in Evanston on the Chicago North Shore, she wanted a stylish crazy quilt "throw" for the day bed in the parlor.

Crazy quilt throws were all the rage, had been since 1876. Belle hadn't made one before but with her skilled fingers, she knew she could. She threaded her short, sharp needle with gold silk floss and with tiny stitches sewed Charles's name on a royal blue satin strip she'd saved in her scrap basket. She'd finally convinced her dignified husband that he should let her copy his signature on the quilt. "Nonsense," he'd huffed, but, of course, he was secretly pleased. She appliquéd a fan of tie silks in the upper righthand corner of the quilt with Charles's name on the center one.

The gray silk moiré piece left over from her Sunday dress would be lovely for her mother-in-law, Mrs. H. A. Reddin, to make a swatch for the quilt. Right in the middle of this square she put her friend Clare Turon's oil painting of a little girl on grosgrain ribbon. She added a piece of raised velvet ribbon from her hat, a scrap of red and green tartan taffeta from her new outfit, and the end of Charles's blue tie with the red embroidery.

It wasn't until 1898 that she got her own mother, Belle Elmina Alling, to sew her name on a length of wide gold satin ribbon when she came to help with the birth of little Louise that year. The quilt wasn't going along very quickly.

In fact, she would never finish it. She asked Clare Turon for another of her charming oil paintings on silk, this time a little girl reaching in a Christmas stocking. Mary J. Munson embroidered lovely carnations in tan and white silk floss on an ecru ribbon. Mrs. J. F. Hesker Detrich boldly stitched her name in red on ice gray satin. Many other friends added pieces, but the century turned, styles changed. She folded away the 38" × 65" unfinished quilt top.

The Hundred-Year-Old Quilt

Several years ago my mother gave me Louise Haynes's handsome antique crazy quilt top. Louise had been my mother's good friend. Eventually she

Fig. 6–1 Louise Haynes's mother made this friendship quilt face in 1892, in
the then-current fashion of parlour crazy quilts made of elegant
fabrics in warm colors.

grew old, ill, and was the last of her line, so she was pleased that my mother valued her quilt. Just before she died she had pulled the unfinished quilt from a trunk and gave it to my mother. I carefully hand sewed a rust colored border on the quilt and hung it in our foyer away from bright light.

This quilt had inspired us to make a friendship quilt for Claudia's wedding, but it only occurred to me to research the quilt when I started this chapter. Mom had few facts. She recalled that Louise's maiden name had been something like "Radin" and said that they'd once driven by the old mansion in Evanston where Louise had lived as a child.

Now I studied the quilt. Ah ha! There's a Reddin, and another! Look how Belle signed her name in two colors to maintain her pre-marital identity. And how Mrs. Reddin Senior, appearing between Charles and Belle, used her formal married name, fitting for a woman of her position in the 1890s.

The scenes of Belle sewing her quilt are conjecture, the result of detective work based on study of the quilt, coupled with what my mother told me. When I first began to sleuth, I wondered if a trail nearly 100 years old would be too cold by now.

I found nearly twenty names on the quilt, noting what colors and types of floss and fabric were used, what designs they sewed or painted, and where they appeared (Fig. 6-2). Knowing Louise's maiden name helped me speculate which might be her husband, her mother-in-law, her mother or her sister, and her grandmother. Will someone in the future ponder over the quilts we make, wondering who we are by the traces we leave?

The quilt has so much to tell. Not only do the names and relationships intrigue, the range of elegant fabrics fascinate, too. From here I went one way, and Linda Otto Lipsett went another. In her book, *Remember Me: Women & Their Friendship Quilts*, (Quilt Digest Press, 1985), she tracked down the descendants of people who made eight old friendship quilts, scoured voluminous records, and reconstructed the lives of these women. This was no easy task. Only heads of households were noted in census listings in the early to mid-1800s. Sometimes the only place a woman's identity survived was written in the family Bible or inscribed on a friendship quilt. A friendship quilt might have been a westward-moving young wife's only link with home, family, and friends. Mrs. Lipsett lists an extensive bibliography for tracing old quilts in her book, along with reams of other historic information. If you'd like to sleuth along this trail, follow some of her leads.

More than the history, it was the luster, texture, and color of the fabrics in Louise's Antique Crazy Quilt that intrigued me. This type of friendship quilt came into vogue around 1876, and its main focus was fabrics. Godey's Ladies Book had been urging Colonial women to use silks and satins in their city parlours, not those plain, folksy cottons. Women were growing more strong-minded in many ways and you could see it on the crazy quilts with brighter colors, random unstructured designs, and elegant fabrics.

Louise's quilt reflected this Victorian era with oil-painted imagery of cherubs, bluebirds, and pansies. The rambling silken embroidery shows different hands—one exquisitely skilled,

Fig. 6–2 Louise's mother, Belle Alling Reddin, embroidered her name and the date on grosgrain ribbon. Her mother-in-law's name appears above on moiré fabric, and her husband Charles's name in the upper right corner on tie silk.

another impatient for quick effect, using all six strands of floss.

Antique Quilt Fabrics

The fabrics. Those incredible fabrics! If you wonder how my crazy quilt could hang there for a couple of years without my reading all the names, it's because I was enamored with the fabrics. My favorite is a brown velvet embroidered with golden-brown stitchery so accurately repeated as to look mechanical, and embellished with dark brown glass seed beads. Some of the embroidered flowers are so exquisite that they may have been cut from imported Chinese silks (Fig. 6–3).

Fabric construction was a high art by the 1890s. The Industrial Revolution was well underway, with spinning and weaving factories in the U.S.A. turning out fine fabrics, competitive with Europe and Asia. My quilt shows elaborate weaves, beyond simple twills and tabbies to complex damask and tapestry designs.

Signatures are stitched on swatches in simple weaves and plain colors in silks and satins. Some of the other fabrics are printed, some woven in complex designs, some are parts of ribbons with raised velvet designs or pre-embroidered silks or velvets, some show the watermark moiré designs, another is a woven silk taffeta plaid. As I search, more unusual fabrics appear. No wonder these ladies wanted to save a bit of each on a quilt to enjoy forever.

Synthetic Fibers

It pained me to add a nylon twill weave fabric as a border for this old quilt. The fabric color and texture were consistent with the 1890s, but nylon's synthetic fibers hadn't been invented yet. One synthetic fiber, however, may be nestled in among the natural silk, linen, wool, and cotton of antique crazy quilts. Rayon was invented in 1884 and called *synthetic silk* until 1924. It was (and is) made from cotton and wood pulp brewed into a liquid and extruded through little holes called spinnarets to form threads. No doubt, this idea came directly from watching spiders and silk worms do the same thing. This technique is still used for modern synthetics, now largely made from petroleum.

This may seem like more than you need to know about fabrics, but it's important to know fabric properties to sew well. For example, iron-on crayon designs will work best on certain synthetic fabrics. The crayon wax and the polyester are both petroleum products and they attract each other. (You've noticed how hard it is to get grease spots out of polyester cloth.)

Synthetics, being largely nonabsorbent, wash and dry quickly. Tough nylon and polyester fabrics can wear like iron. They're so strong, they are used in tire treads, for fishing line, and strapping tapes.

When the use of synthetic fibers hit its zenith in the 1960s, natural fibers were eclipsed in popularity. After all, synthetics washed better, wore longer, cost less, didn't fade, didn't wrinkle, and had other labor- and cost-saving advantages. Everyone made everything from synthetics—clothing, carpets, furry toys, linens, upholstery, then dishes, auto parts, buckets, mops—everything.

Fig. 6–3 Note the variety of hand-embroidery stitches on Louise's Quilt, accentuating the various fabric patches, from silk and linen to fine cotton and lightweight wool.

The first synthetic fibers weren't very soft to touch, were hot to wear on a sticky day, and held onto grease spots. So textile engineers and designers examined natural fibers to see why they were better, and then added crimps, hollow centers, different extruded shapes, and more improvements to synthetic fibers to achieve softness, loft, absorbency, and other natural qualities.

Eventually, when oil prices sent the cost of synthetics up and fashion designers rediscovered natural fibers, the tide turned. But today's naturals aren't the presynthetic naturals. Now, technology developed for synthetics is applied to naturals and even better natural fabrics result, with fewer wrinkles and more permanent dyes. Some of the best fabrics combine both natural and synthetic fibers. Of special interest to quilters are the cotton-polyester blends. Other books may insist that only pure cottons will do (they usually hand-sew better). Try them all and see what you like best.

Characteristics of Suitable Fabrics

Your best aid in judging fabrics is the hang tag or printed text on the fabric bolt: fabric content, width, weave, type, shrinkage, color fastness, washability, and ironing temperature are all important in quiltmaking. Ideally, you'd copy this information and pin it to the fabric you buy. In practice, you may choose to buy only preshrunk, washable fabrics and not worry.

Color

First, of course, a quilter searches for just the right colors. Shop for all the fabric you need within a short span of time so related colors are still available. Don't worry too much about color trends and current style. Choose colors you really like rather than what's trendy. If all the colors in a room are keyed to each other, changing styles won't matter. Further, quilts are made to last and can reappear when their colors come around again.

Test fabrics for permanent color. To see if the dye "crocks" or rubs off, wad the fabric you are considering and rub it on a piece of white sheeting. If color comes off, the dye is not permanent or too much remains in the fabric. Some dyes, like cotton madras, may not crock but will run in hot water. When in doubt, test fabric for color fastness in hot water.

Texture and Weight

"Hand" is the name given to how the fabric feels as it flexes and drapes. A soft cotton fabric will have a different hand when printed with stiff textile dyes. Hand is affected by the type of fiber, the weave of the fabric, the applied design, and the weight and density of the fibers. Feel the fabrics as you shop.

Soft hand matters most for hand stitchers. You need a lightweight, flexible, firmly woven, soft-weave fabric to hand sew and quilt. Calico, percale, and other cotton or cotton-polyester tabby weave fabrics are best. All you need is one tightly woven broadcloth in your quilt to slow your needle and ruin your fingers. Try to choose soft fabrics, all the same weight, for your hand-sewn quilt. (I rarely manage this, since I go for color first, but you know that old "do as I say, not as I do" advice.)

Machine stitchers can use a greater

Fig. 6–4 Soft machine-embroidery threads enhance the rich fabrics in this detail of a machine-stitched crazy quilt.

variety. Tightly woven broadcloth is ideal for appliqué because it won't fray much and will hold its shape while being stitched. For background fabrics, even heavier fibers and tight weaves are best so the machine satin stitching will not pucker the fabric.

On a pieced quilt, it's best to use all the same weight fabrics so one does not pull another out of shape. Pieced quilts require great accuracy, so using fabrics of the same weight and texture helps. On authentic crazy quilts, many marvelous, unusual, and fragile fabrics can be used because backing fabric supports them.

Modern day machine stitchers are free to use any wild and wonderful combination of fabrics on their quilts.

The mechanical force of the sewing machine rams the needle through almost everything. With fine fabrics and good care, your creations can last more than a lifetime.

Care

The care needed for different fabrics may affect which ones you choose. For example, you'll need to press a quilt while making it, so putting a low ironing-temperature silk right next to a high ironing-temperature linen creates problems. These pieces may suffer a fate similar to that of some old quilts in which silk pieces disintegrate with age and heat. If you use fabrics with varying ironing temperatures adjacent to one another, always use a pressing cloth and steam iron.

Many fabrics fresh from the mill have been stretched, pressed, coated with filler, mercerized, or given other treatments to create a pleasing surface. Because of this, and due to the wear and tear of the washing process, many fabrics lose their crispness after washing.

All quilting books urge you to wash fabrics first. This ensures that any shrinkage will occur before fabrics are stitched—instead of later, when it might distort the completed quilt. Washing removes fillers, compression from pressing, and distortions, leaving

Fig. 6–5 Contemporary block makers might use any fabric. Sally Risberg used fluffy terrycloth for snow on a block for Gini's Wedding Quilt.

a softer fabric. It also lets you know which colors will run, and allows you to "set" these colors with hot water and vinegar.

I usually don't plan to wash my machine-sewn creations, especially something as special and varied in content as a friendship quilt (some people who contribute squares glue things on). Washing is apt to pucker the stitching, and it alters the character of the fabrics. Washing often affects "rich" fabrics such as taffeta, moiré, lamé, silk, and wool fabrics, and it alters cottons, too. I usually try to shop carefully and avoid problem fabrics.

Most fabrics, unless they are very light colors, will not need washing, especially in a keepsake quilt. To maintain the original freshness, good care (avoiding daily use, pets, peanut butter sandwiches, bright sunshine) and brushing will help keep quilts clean.

Modern washing machines, dryers, and synthetic fabrics are made for each other—but not for handmade quilts. If you must, wash your quilt with extra care in tepid water and air dry. Of course, you can wash everyday quilts in a washing machine. For these, choose cotton blends and machine sew them quilt-in-a-day style in exuberant colors and giant-sized patches. Save your friendship quilts for keepsakes.

Stability

Background fabrics must be stable and woven firmly enough to keep their shapes. They must be firm and heavy enough to apply other fabrics and be machine embroidered, yet soft enough to hand sew. Not easy! You can increase fabric stability by adding a backing fabric or a removable paper back-

Louise's Antique Crazy Quilt

Claudia's Wedding Quilt

The Minister's Retirement Quilt

Kim's Valentine Quilt

The Trenton Quilt, 1839

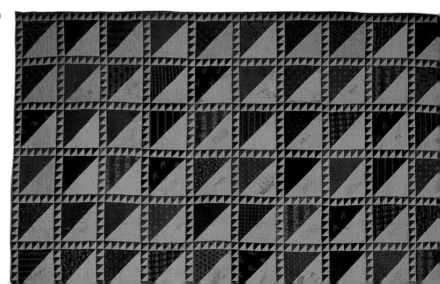

Peter's Wedding Quilt

Lori's Wedding Quilt

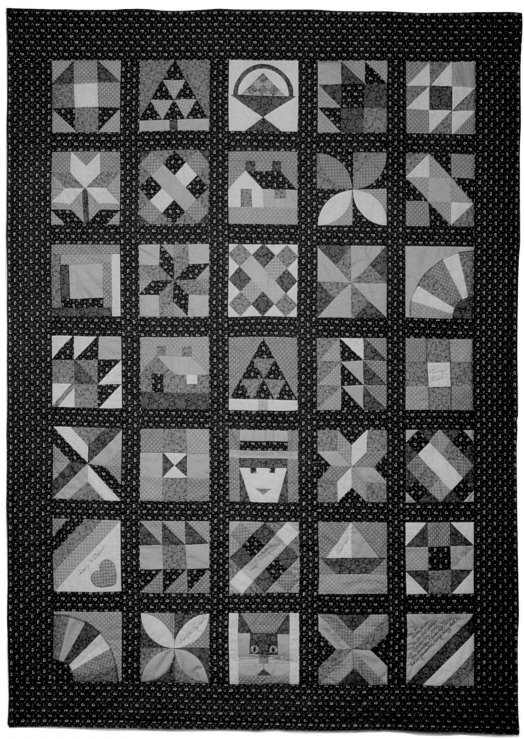

Hattie's Birthday Quilt

The Artists' Quilt

Janet's Baby Quilt

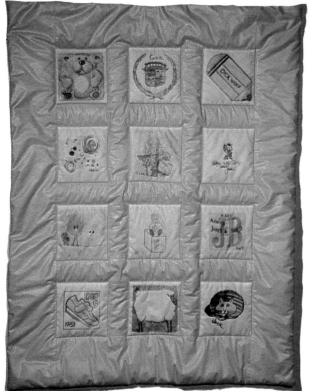

ing can be used. (See Chapter 8 on machine appliqué for details.)

Always feel the fabrics you plan to buy. If you aren't lucky enough to live near a good fabric store, consult the ads in quilting and fabric magazines for mail-order fabrics. Some will send swatches; a few of these places are listed in Sources of Supply.

Keep in mind what the fabric has to do and how it handles when you are shopping. This advice sounds easy to follow, but wait until you get to the fabric store and fall in love with a beautiful color . . . in the wrong fabric!

I've been working with fabrics forever and I still choose the wrong one sometimes. For Lori's Wedding Quilt, I chose a lightweight, unbleached muslin for its homespun character to use as the background square. Unfortunately, since this particular fabric is the standard one used for crazy quilt backings, most people thought it was supposed to be totally covered and added other fabric colors (which altered the color scheme). I mention this mistake right off, so you'll know you're among friends if you choose an inappropriate or difficult fabric to work with.

Grain

Grain refers to the direction of the warp and weft threads in the fabric. Warp threads, the strongest and longest threads, are strung on the loom and run lengthwise, parallel to the selvage. They must be strong to resist the constant abrasion as the loom moves the warp threads up and down so the filler (weft) threads can be woven in place. These warp threads are stretched dur-

ing weaving and will be the most apt to shrink in washing.

Sometimes fabric is pulled out-of-square, or off-grain, on the rollers as it is woven at the mill. Be careful in cutting blocks from off-grain fabric. To check the grain, tear fabric across the width or pull a thread across to see if it is "square." If not, grasp the "shorter" opposite corners and pull firmly to straighten. Press the fabric to keep it true-grained.

You can also true the fabric by washing and ironing it. You *cannot* straighten a fabric successfully when a geometric or linear design is printed on off-grain fabric at the mill. Check for this fault when buying geometric patterns such as polka dots, grids, or stripes.

Tearing Fabrics

For a friendship quilt that is to be pieced or appliquéd, quilt fabrics should cut or tear well, since you will need to divide the fabric into so many small pieces. The advantages of tearing are several: it will put the fabric "on-grain," the pieces will be the same width, and it goes quickly. The disadvantages are: tearing may pull threads and pucker or curl the fabric, a fabric may not tear straight, or it may not tear at all. Cotton fabrics usually tear best. Don't try tearing twills, brocades, polyesters, or laces, for example, since you can never tell what they will do.

The Right Stuff

Traditionally, certain quilt types are made in characteristic fabrics. These standards are discussed below, but only as a guide. Many imaginative choices of fabric can succeed.

Fig. 6–6 Claudia Stroud used the traditional small-print soft cotton fabrics preferred by quiltmakers for easy handling, long wear, and good appearance.

1. Hand-sewn pieced or appliquéd quilts

Use all the same weight and texture of fabrics in a firm, plain weave, light-weight, soft 100% cotton. For appliqué pieces, choose fabrics that can be hemmed and don't fray too badly (no loose weaves).

Typical fabric: Small prints and solid colors in percale, calico, muslin, chintz, quilting cotton.

Other possible fabrics: Soft-weave cotton-polyester broadcloth, gingham, medium-weight silks, chambray, lightweight wool.

2. Machine-sewn pieced quilt blocks

Use all the same weight and texture of fabric in plain weave, medium-weight fabric. For appliqué pieces, choose fabrics that don't fray too badly (are tightly woven).

Typical fabric: Small prints and solid colors in soft, 100% cotton, such as percale, calico, muslin, chintz, quilting cotton. The weave may be firmer than for hand sewing.

Other possible fabrics: Cotton-polyester broadcloth, gingham, cotton sheeting, medium-weight silks, chambray, lightweight wool, ticking, lightweight denim, sailcloth. Choose small prints and plain colors.

3. Machine-sewn appliqué

Use a medium-weight, firmly woven background fabric. Add backing to stabilize if necessary. For the applied pieces, use firmly woven fabrics that do not fray badly.

Suitable backing fabric: Broadcloth, chintz, glazed chintz, lightweight canvas, denim, piqué, ticking.

Suitable applied fabrics: Glazed chintz in solids or prints, broadcloth, lightweight canvas, piqué, ticking, cotton-polyester broadcloth, gingham, cotton sheeting, medium-weight silk, chambray, lightweight wool, lightweight denim, sailcloth.

Other possible fabrics: A group of wool and wool-blend fabrics; a related group of fabrics with sheen, such as brocades, taffetas, lamés; textured fabrics in corduroy, velvet, lace, and ribbon may also be used—indeed, almost any fabric can be applied onto another by machine.

4. Crazy quilt patchwork

For a Victorian type crazy quilt, use muslin backing for all fabrics.

Typical quilt face fabrics: Elegant silks and velvets, moirés, and ribbons.

Also suitable: Silky polyester fabrics; soft, frayable fabrics can be used with a wide hem; laces and open weaves used over a silky backing.

Decorative embroidery: Hand or machine embroider with shiny threads.

For a Country-style crazy quilt, use fabric with no sheen such as lightweight wool, twill, crepe, tweed, plain and print colors. Use muslin for backing. Hand or machine embroider with cotton or wool embroidery floss.

5. Cross-stitch

For counted cross-stitch, use cloth with specified thread count (12 stitches per inch, for example). For iron-on transfer cross-stitch to be worked by hand, use soft weave cotton fabric. Use an embroidery hoop.

Typical fabrics: Percale, calico, gingham, sheeting, or linen for hand embroidery. For sewing machine cross-stitch, use firmly woven medium-weight cotton, cotton blend, or linen fabric. Use a machine embroidery hoop.

6. Crayon transfer blocks

Use plain weave, firmly woven glazed chintz (resin coated) or polyester fabrics. Test a small piece to see how well the color adheres.

7. Painting or dyeing blocks

For acrylic, oil, or textile paints, use cotton, cotton-poly blends, silk in a firmly woven tabby weave.

For dyes, use natural fibers, all cotton, all silk, wool, or linen. Or use special dyes for synthetics.

8. Machine-embroidered blocks

Use a firmly woven, medium-weight background fabric. Use backing if necessary. Use a machine embroidery hoop if necessary. Use preshrunk thread.

Suitable fabrics: Broadcloth, sailcloth, linen, canvas, sheeting, piqué, organdy.

9. Hand-embroidered blocks

Use soft, lightweight cotton, cotton blend, silk, or linen fabric. Use heavy enough weight so threads do not "shadow" unless you are aiming for this effect.

Suitable fabrics: Lawn, percale, linen, silks, some broadcloth.

10. Added decorations and trims

Use background fabric the same weight as—or heavier than—the applied decorations.

Suitable trims: Ribbons, beads, buttons, sequins, fake furs, preembroidered emblems.

Louise's Antique Crazy Quilt

QUILT PROFILE

OCCASION AND GROUP: Made in the 1890s to collect and display friends' and relatives' signatures

QUILT DESIGNER: Belle Alling Reddin

THEME: Victorian-era crazy quilt of elegant fabrics and ribbons with sentimental value. Includes signatures, embroidery, and small paintings.

ORGANIZATION: Friends sewed their names on patches, or Belle collected their signatures and embroidered them herself

TECHNIQUE: Unstructured design of random-shaped patches, appliquéd to a muslin backing. All raw edges are hemmed or covered with another patch so no backing shows. Patches are held in place with concealed hand stitching, then hand embroidered. Silk embroidery flosses in assorted colors outline each patch with decorative embroidery stitches. Additional decorative motifs, such as paintings and beautifully embroidered flowers, appear on patches.

TIME: Dates on Louise's Antique Crazy quilt are 1892 to 1898.

SIZE: 47½″ × 72½″

BLOCKS: 12½″ squares

LAYOUT: 15 blocks, 3 across and 5 vertical, 5″ borders

COLORS: Typical of clothing of the 1890s, colors range from white, ecru, light gray, soft gold, yellow, and tan to red, brown, purple, grayed blue, dark blue, maroon, and black. The modern border added is deep rust.

FABRICS: The widest possible assortment of silk, cotton, wool, and linen. These include high- and low-cut velvet, printed velvet, beaded velveteen, velvet ribbon, handkerchief-weight silk, moiré silk, twill silk, rib cord silk, brocade silk, printed silk, award ribbons, grosgrain ribbon, double-weave damask (linen), faille, crepe, tie silks in jacquard weaves, and others.

YARDAGE: About 9⅛ yards of assorted fabrics

QUILTING METHOD: Crazy quilts are commonly yarn-knotted at 6″ intervals related to the squares.

DISPLAY: The border has a rod slot. The quilt is displayed in my foyer out of bright light and heat (see color insert).

Making a Contemporary Crazy Quilt

MATERIALS

(Buy extra fabric for safety margin)

Quilt face: 100 to 300 swatches of assorted elegant fabrics	3	yards
Block linings: 15 blocks, 14″ squares	2	yards
Border and backing	4⅛	yards
2 strips, 24½″ × 73½″, for backing		
2 strips, 5″ × 73½″, for side borders		
2 strips, 5″ × 49″, for top and bottom borders		
Total	9⅛	yards

Filler: 48″ × 75″ preshrunk blanket or cotton flannel
Other supplies: assorted harmonizing colors of embroidery floss in silk or rayon for quilts needing sheen; cotton or wool floss for other fabrics; machine sewing thread to match the border; hand-sewing thread; scissors, pins, embroidery hoop

PROCEDURE

Assembling Face Fabrics

Collect and assemble the widest possible range of fabrics. Fabrics should relate in color, texture, and type. Following are several possibilities for crazy quilts.

1. Choose elegant silks, velvets, and similar lustrous fabrics for a Victorian city parlour look. Balance bright colors with equal amounts — or more — of light, dark, and muted colors; avoid harsh colors like bright green and hot pink.

2. Select homespun fabrics, warmly colored and textured in wools, tweeds, twills, and cords for a Country look.

3. Choose cotton calicos and percales in small prints, and solid colors closely related in color range.

4. Use swatches of all your favorite old dresses, ribbons, silk scarves, hat bands, men's ties, or award ribbons.

Laying Out the Top

Lay the colors out on the floor, table, or bed, all touching each other so you can see what looks good, what just doesn't go, and what you need more of. Crazy quilts look random but successful ones are actually carefully assembled like a jigsaw puzzle.

If possible, choose the border and backing colors before you plan the quilt face. If not, take the completed quilt face to the fabric store and search until you find the right border. As an advocate of planning ahead, I hate to admit how often I do this.

Making the Blocks

1. Select about 20 patches of face fabrics to be appliquéd to each lining

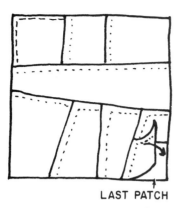

LAST PATCH

Fig. 6–7 To make appliquéd crazy quilt patches, overlap hemmed patches on the lining block so no raw edges result.

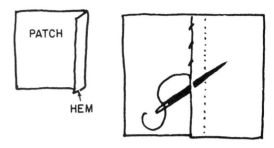

Fig. 6–8 Fold a hem where one patch overlaps another, then hand-sew hemmed edges with hidden stitches.

block. Except for ribbons with finished edges, plan at least ¼″ seam allowance around each patch to be turned back in a hem or overlaid by another piece.

2. Lay the patches on the block, overlapping each other in random patterns to completely cover the backing all the way to the edges. This includes a ½″ seam allowance around the backing block (Fig. 6–7). If you wish, lay out all the blocks at once to see how they look together.

3. While fitting patches, keep in mind how you will sew them to the lining. (See instructions for hand and machine sewing below.) Beginning in one corner, lay each patch overlapping the previous one, like fish scales, working toward the opposite corner (Fig. 6–7). Keep adjoining edges straight so they will be easier to hem and to sew. Louise's Antique Crazy Quilt is made in squares, but patches overlap and obscure some seam lines. These patches were added to cover raw edges after assembling the squares and before embroidering.

Hand-Sewing Blocks

1. When you achieve a block design you like, fold and finger-press or iron a ¼″ hem on each patch that overlaps another (Fig. 6–8).

2. Insert silk pins to hold hems and patches in place. If any backing shows, rearrange patches to cover it.

3. Use a fine needle and hidden stitching (Fig. 6–8) to sew each patch in place.

4. Continue appliquéing quilt-face patches onto all fifteen blocks.

5. Most of the decorative embroidery can be done now, on individual blocks, which makes it easier.

Machine-Sewing Blocks

You may also use this method for hand sewing, but it was designed for fast machine construction.

1. When you achieve a block design you like, transfer the first corner patch to another lining block and topstitch it in place along the lining edge in the seam allowance (Fig. 6–9A).

2. Finger-fold (or press) a hem in the next overlapping patch and lay it on the first, overlapping the raw edge. Pin baste it in place by inserting silk pins

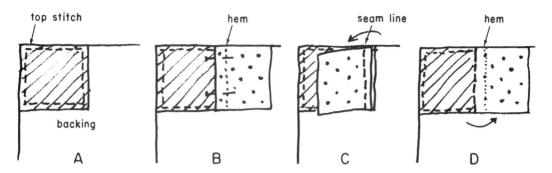

Fig. 6–9 Machine stitching a crazy quilt. A. Topstitch the first block in place. B. Fold a hem in the overlapping block and pin. C. Lay second patch on first, unfold pinned hem, and machine sew. D. To reposition second piece, refold hem and press.

at right angles into the hem fold and into the lining (Fig. 6–9B).

3. Unfold the patch along the hem line and lay it face-to-face with the first patch. Remove pins now hidden by top patch and reposition along the hem line. Machine stitch along the hem fold line (Fig. 6–9C).

4. Refold the second patch, press, and pin it to the backing (Fig. 6–9D). This results in a concealed seam. Continue adding patches in this same manner.

Concealing Raw Edges

If an added patch ends *within* the block, you have several choices for concealing the raw edge. Try one of the six suggestions that follow:

- Overlap with an additional patch (Fig. 6–10A)
- For overlapping patches, fold a hem along the second raw edge before folding the stitching hem line (Fig. 6–10B). Fold and stitch the hem line; unfold; press and pin in place; then hand or machine topstitch the second folded hem in place.
- Join two overlapping patches with a

seam before hemming. To do this, finger-fold a hem in the top patch where it overlaps the other. Right-angle pin through the hem line into the other patch to establish the stitch line. Unfold so the hemmed patch is face-to-face with the other patch and sew this seam. Open the joined patches, fold a hem, and join to the block as in Figure 6–10 B, C, and D.

- For a "fan," you can seam all the patches together except the rounded center before applying it to the block (Fig. 6–10D). Overlap its raw edges with other patches or, if it overlaps, hem the raw edges and topstitch it in place.
- For a final patch, or a rounded patch, finger-fold or press a hem on all overlapping edges. On a rounded patch, soft fabric may hem easily, but stiffer fabrics may require running a basting thread to gather the hem evenly, then press. If necessary, cut notches in the hem to eliminate extra fabric. Pin the patch in place and machine topstitch or hand-sew (Fig. 6–10E). Stitching can be covered later by embroidery.

87

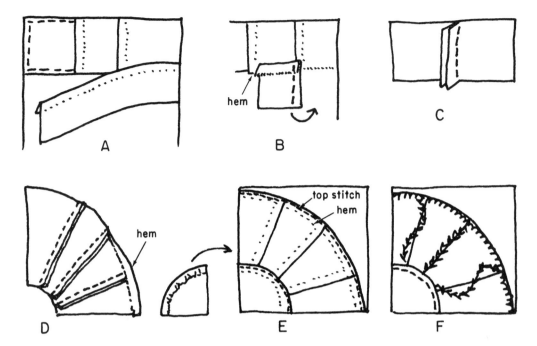

Fig. 6–10 To cover raw edges, try one of these methods: A. Overlap with added patch; B. hem overlapping edge before sewing a patch in place; C. sew two adjoining patches before stitching to backing block; D. seam several pieces together and hem; E. add a final hemmed piece, then topstitch to backing; F. use decorative hand or machine embroidery to embellish and anchor quilt patches.

• Hand or machine embroider decorative stitching (Fig. 6–10F). If your machine has automatic feather stitch, buttonhole stitch, and other "hand embroidery" stitches, use heavy machine embroidery thread to sew designs. Vary the width and length of stitch for a hand-controlled look. If your machine does not have automatic stitches, but you have good dexterity, "free sew" by machine, using straight and zigzag stitching to look like hand embroidery. (For embroidery details, see Chapter 9).

Assembling the Quilt

1. Crazy quilt blocks are joined directly, with no sashing. Join blocks into rows, then join rows. Some quilts have patches applied after seaming the blocks together. These may overlap and obscure the seams, as in Louise's Antique Crazy Quilt.

2. Embroider the blocks before or after seaming them. Embroider seams after assembly. Join the borders.

3. Crazy quilts usually have a very thin filler, and are quilted with yarn knots at 6" intervals. (See Chapter 12 for a variety of finishing techniques.)

Chapter 7

Tools for Patchwork

Hattie's Birthday Quilt

The phrase "drafting a pattern" means using drafting tools and techniques to make an accurate pattern. That's why Hattie's patchwork quilt is paired with information on drafting materials and quilting supplies. This chapter also includes information on pieced blocks, ways to invent your own block designs, and how to make Hattie's Birthday Quilt.

To celebrate my granddaughter Hattie's first birthday, I decided to make her a grown-up keepsake, an authentic friendship quilt. I was to make all the patches, while her mother Claudia collected friends' signatures for the quilt.

Many of the first friendship quilts in the 1840s were made this way. Women in those days asked their friends and relatives to sign a plain cotton fabric patch in ink, or to sign a slip of paper to be copied in flowing script on fabric patches (after the invention of a better ink that did not cause fabric to deteriorate). They combined the signed patches with everyday fabric scraps into pieced blocks (just as often called squares). These first friendship quilts were usually limited to the same pieced pattern throughout. The Trenton Quilt (Fig. 7–2) is an example of the repeated motif. "Album Block" was a popular pattern, used again and again in early quilts. Hattie's quilt has twenty different patterns or variations, including four "Album Blocks." These four all look different (see Fig. 7–1 and color section) because of color changes, one of the magics of quilting.

Most of Hattie's blocks are traditional pieced designs. Although the term *patchwork* applies to any quilt in this book since all are assembled from pieces, people usually assume this means pieced quilts only. Piecing generally means making quilt blocks from fabric patches seamed together without a background square.

Quiltmaking Tools and How to Use Them

Accuracy is vitally important in making pieced blocks. Pieced block patterns are all based on straight lines and curves; original designs will be most successful if you maintain this simplified geometric approach.

Some block designs that look easy to assemble aren't, mainly because three seams come together at an angle. A prime example of this is the "Star." Unless you divide the edge triangles, there's no way to speed this one up by

Fig. 7–1 Hattie Stroud's first birthday quilt has traditional pieced-block patterns, along with
some original ones, in soft and dark greens, soft blue, muted pink,
rusty red, and ecru.

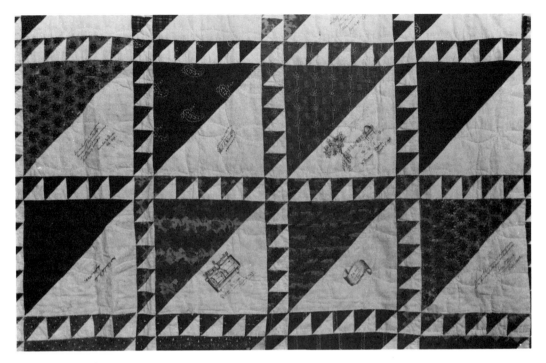

Fig. 7–2 The Trenton Quilt consists of traditional, identical pattern blocks in similar red-toned print fabrics. Quilting stitches are an all-over daisy pattern. Patches show sayings and scenes in the 1830s; blocks were signed in ink before the quilt was pieced.

combining units for nice long seams, as with most of Hattie's blocks. So, when choosing pieced patterns or creating your own, watch for intersections with angles.

Pieced patterns can be made any size, for 6″ squares to 16″ squares (or larger), so it helps to know how to draft patterns and change pattern sizes.

Many tools can be found in stores that stock school, art, or office supplies. For sewing supplies, search fabric stores, sewing departments, quilt magazine ads, and sewing supply catalogs. I've included the basics, added items used to make Hattie's quilt, and suggested substitutes.

Measuring and Computing Aids

Tape Measure: You'll need a flexible tape measure 60″ long (1.5 meters). Tape measures get lots of wear (including a romp with the cat), so buy a good non-stretch, plastic-coated fabric tape with metal tip ends.

Ruler and Yardstick: Choose a 12″ or 15″ straight-edge ruler for drafting patterns and for marking straight seam lines on the back of fabric. You'll also need a wood or metal yardstick for drawing long straight seam lines on fabric.

Calculator: I use my small electronic calculator to figure the finished width and length of quilts with different numbers or sizes of squares; to figure fabric amounts; to compute fabric costs; and to divide distances on patterns into parts when pattern drafting or enlarging. (Chapter 3 includes a conversion chart for changing the calculator's decimals to fractions and percentages.)

Guides: These come in clear plastic in a variety of shapes, including triangles in 45° or 30°–60°, and panels of assorted-size circles, ovals, and other geometric shapes. Use the square corner of the triangle for right angles, and the angle for diagonal lines. For circles and arcs, use the circle guide or a compass. Lacking these, you can use a dish, a roll of tape, or anything that's round and the correct size to trace.

T-square: This is a combination ruler and guide. My favorite is a 12″ white plastic T-square found in a stationery store. To use it as a guide for drawing straight parallel lines, fit the T end to the side of your drawing board or pad of paper, then slide it up or down for subsequent parallel lines. To draw lines at right angles, (corners of true squares), fit the T-square to slide along the bottom edge of the drawing board, or use a triangle to slide along the T-square (Fig. 7–3). (*Note:* Board or pad must be square to get accurate results.)

Drawing and Pattern-Making Supplies

Graph Paper: Graph paper is useful for all phases of quilt planning, from making the patchwork designs, to planning the quilt layout, to computing fabric amounts by layout. It comes in 8½″ × 11″ pads of 25 or more sheets, or in larger sheets, and in dif-

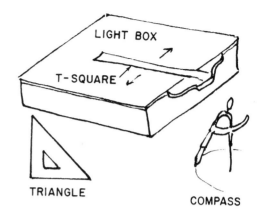

Fig. 7–3 Drafting tools for quilters.

ferent square sizes: ¼″, ⅛″, or ¹⁄₁₀″, or metric measurements.

Tracing Paper: This translucent paper allows you to trace signatures, and pattern pieces, or make changes in a design. You can also use it as an overlay for machine stitching or as a stabilizer for machine appliqué (see Chapter 8). Tracing paper comes as a thin onion skin, or as a heavier weight less apt to tear when erased or sewn through. Rolls are usually more economical than tablets.

Sketching and Backing Paper: I use plain typing paper to sketch ideas, to make preliminary quilt block designs, to back fabric while stitching, or to overlay my design on the fabric face as a stitching guide. Because I use so much, I buy inexpensive photocopy or mimeograph paper in 500–sheet packages at office supply stores. (And watch for sales. I got a ream of green copy paper for 17% off on St. Patrick's Day. Weird but handy.) Some thrifty people, including me, use newspaper or used paper as backing, but be careful that printing ink doesn't transfer.

Template Cardboard: Stiff quilt

block patterns (templates) work best for tracing around, so use "cover stock" paper or cardboard to make them. Some of the best cardboard comes as backing for paper pads or new shirt packaging. If you plan to use the templates often, make them of clear or translucent plastic. (Or buy commercial templates.)

Marking Pencils: Use No. 2 pencils for drawing on paper and for marking medium to light-colored fabric backs. Draw on fabric *back only* and then lightly, since some marks won't wash out. For marking fabric faces, use blue tailor's chalk pencils on white or light fabrics, and white for darker ones. Everyone keeps searching for the perfect marking device. Some new inventions include pens whose marks disappear and white pencil lines that wash out. See notions sections and sewing catalogs for these new ideas.

Marking pens: Every time I use pens to mark fabrics, I'm sorry I did. The ink does not come out if you make a mistake, it fades in time so it's not permanent enough to be used as surface design, and it may bleed into other colors or smear off during the stitching. Because they are so handy, some people use markers to draw cutting lines on fabric, and cut just inside the ink line, but I recommend light pencil or tailor's chalk.

Colored Pencils: Consider investing in a set of Prismacolor Thick Lead Art Set pencils. These wax-based soft colored pencils have bright colors that cover well, do not run when wet, but will wash out in hot water. Draw lightly on fabric, since it may smear. The less expensive, hard thin-lead colored pencils are water-soluble and may bleed or run. You can use them many ways: different colors help distinguish one line from another when making pattern alterations; you can try various color schemes on graph paper before buying fabric; or use appropriate colors to mark fabric.

Erasers: Use a clean, soft red eraser on paper and a gum eraser on fabric. If needed, use artist's white-out to cover ink-drawn lines on paper. I wash quilts as little as possible to maintain the finish, so I avoid lines on fabric surfaces at all costs.

Light Box (portable tracing box): A light box has a translucent white plastic top, illuminated from within. It can be used for many purposes: tracing designs, making changes, copying signatures, lining up fabric appliqué pieces, or viewing slides. Commercial light boxes, like my Seerite, are expensive, but you can make your own (Fig. 7–4). For a convenient size, buy a 16" × 18" piece of ¼"-thick translucent white plastic from a glass or building supply store. Make a frame of 1" × 4" pine, 16" × 18" × 4" high. Glue or screw the plastic to the top edge of the frame.

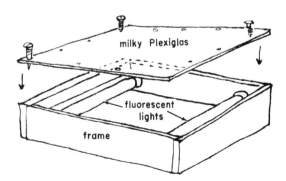

milky Plexiglas
fluorescent lights
frame

Fig. 7–4 A homemade light box provides good light for tracing. Use a four-board frame, two fluorescent tube lights, translucent Plexiglas top.

Mount two small fluorescent tubes inside (under-shelf light kits work fine) or just set the light box over the lights. If you have only occasional need for tracing, try taping tracing paper over the design on a window so the backlight illuminates the lines, or use a glass-top table. Robbie Fanning says to go outside at night to trace on a window for back-lighting, but make sure the window is clean.

Opaque Projector: If you do a lot of scaling up and down, this is a useful tool. It's quicker and easier than scaling by graph. Two versions are available: (1) An inexpensive children's toy version that is placed over the design to be traced — for increased magnification, you can extend the lens by making a cardboard tube around it; and (2) a projector available from Seerite requires placing the design face-down on top — it's not as easy to use, but has a better lens, and a reducing lens is available.

Cutting Tools

I'm so fond of scissors that I keep a pair of stork-shaped embroidery scissors in my purse tied by string to the purse handle. It doesn't matter how many pairs you have — some days you won't be able to find a single one. Here's a list of my other favorite kinds to have on hand.

Dressmaker's Shears: Standard shears are 8" to 10" long. Due to their popularity, they come in many permutations: for example, with lightweight plastic handles angled for thumb and fingers, and for right and left hands. Shears are used for general fabric cutting and are long enough to cut a straight line easily. Get a good pair for yourself and another for the rest of the family. Hide yours so they won't get lost, dropped, left out in the rain, used as a screwdriver, or wire cutter.

Embroidery Scissors: These 4" to 6" scissors have sharp points and narrow blades, ideal for hand sewing or cutting out intricate appliqués. Buy a quality pair, since inexpensive ones don't cut well. Hide these, too.

Clippers: Clippers come in two main styles, pencil-shaped or hand-fitted with a finger loop to swing out of the way when not in use. Both have two short, sharp blades you squeeze together to clip threads — quicker than getting into the scissors finger holes.

Appliqué Scissors: These Gingher scissors have one narrow and one half-moon-shaped blade. While you can trim machine appliqué with embroidery scissors, appliqué scissors allow you to trim without cutting the backing fabric, to grade seams, and to trim close to edge stitching.

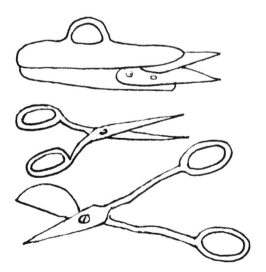

Fig. 7–5 From top, clippers; 4" sewing scissors; appliqué scissors.

Paper Cutter: What a great day when I discovered I could cut fabric strips and patchwork patches on my paper cutter. The ½" grid on the wooden measuring board helps measure sizes, and the blade shears off a neat straight line, eliminating frayed edges from tearing. It will cut more than one layer of fabric, depending on the fabric type, so you can use it to trim seams and cut multiples. Be sure to align fabric along the grain and hold fabric firmly or it will pull, making it out of square. Of course, it also cuts paper for patterns and designs, and cardboard templates too. Like scissors and shears, it will need occasional sharpening.

Knife Blades: If you plan to make cardboard or plastic "window" templates, you'll need an X-acto knife and box of fresh sharp blades. Many people love a rotary cutting wheel. A cutting board for cutting single and multiple layers is available to protect table tops. Remember to slide the blade cover in place after each use.

Seam Ripper: Last among the cutters but not least, you must own a seam ripper to take out sewing machine stitching. Accuracy may be admirable elsewhere, but in piecing a quilt it is *mandatory*. I use my seam ripper more than I like to admit to remove stitching and readjust seams until they're correct.

Gluing and Pinning

Nothing improved the quality and ease of machine appliqué like the invention of various adhesives to keep the pieces in place while stitching. Here are the ones I use most.

Baste and Glue Stick: Similar to the glue stick used for paper crafts, the baste and glue stick comes in a lipstick-size tube of glue. It holds appliqué pieces, seams, lace, and even buttons in place for stitching, then washes out or dries. Don't use too much or it will gum up the machine needle. Watch for black mildew spots on used glue sticks. Some spray-on adhesives are available, but be sure the room is well-ventilated when you use them. There's a new Teflon adhesive sheet, but I haven't tried it yet.

Adhesive Backings: These come by the yard in fabric stores. Stitch Witchery is a lacy, dry adhesive sheet applied to fabric backs, or laid between fabrics and bonded with the heat of an iron. (Careful! It sticks to iron faceplates, too.) Another is a non-woven facing with dry adhesive on one side, used as backing to stabilize and thicken other fabrics. This now comes with quilt patches printed on it, or you can draw your own patch piece or appliqué design on it.

Sticky Adhesives: Most commonly, these products are used for non-sewn hems. They are not reusable, so must be applied accurately, and they do thicken the "seam," but are fast and handy.

Pins: I use three kinds of pins: fine, sharp dressmaker's pins for appliqué pieces; 1½" glass-headed pins for pinning quilt seams and layers; and safety pins for holding the quilt layers firmly together while machine quilting. If you use brass pins, keep them clean so they won't leave marks.

Sewing Supplies

Needles: Use fine sharp or quilting needles (called betweens) for hand-sewing pieced quilt blocks, sizes 6 or 7.

I use a size 3 or 6 Talon crewel embroidery needle because the long eye is easier to thread. Use a larger, longer needle for basting.

Threads; Fit the thread to the type of work or material, and fit the needle to the thread. For hand-sewing quilts, use fine quality quilting thread that won't untwist or tangle, or draw size 50 Mercerized cotton thread through a beeswax block. For lightweight fabrics, use fine threads to hand or machine sew. For strength, use good quality poly-cotton threads. For sheen, use rayon or silk threads, and machine-sew more slowly, so they don't break. For economy, buy thread in larger quantities on cones. For more details on threads (and a million other useful ideas) see Robbie and Tony Fanning's *The Complete Book of Machine Embroidery* (Chilton, 1986).

Thread Holder: This heavy metal base, with 18″ metal rod and eye, feeds cone thread to your sewing machine and avoids tangles.

Thimbles: I can't believe I've never learned to use a thimble; you really should for hand sewing of any duration. Leather thimbles may feel and work better than metal ones. I sometimes keep small pliers on hand to pull stubborn needles through. Robbie uses a deflated balloon.

Sewing Machine: Yes, any working machine—even an old straight-stitch treadle—will do many of the jobs required in this book. An old timer can be fitted with a darning foot for free-motion sewing. For machine appliqué, you'll need a swing needle machine that can zigzag. And once you go this far, you'll want one that doesn't jam, that backstitches, sews quietly, and has other fancy stitches like the feather-stitch. There's no end. Just like cars, there's always a glossier model in the showroom. And I keep wanting it. Consider your needs and buy accordingly. Also consult with the most reputable and closest repair service for recommendations on brands.

Miscellaneous Supplies

Irons and Pressing: Buy a good steam iron, keep the faceplate clean, and never drop it. Some of the small hand steamers are useful for taking

Fig. 7–6 "Hattie's Hat," a pieced block pattern created especially for my granddaughter, Hattie Elizabeth Stroud, in the simplified geometric style characteristic of patchwork quilts.

out wrinkles. My new tailor's presser is fine for crayon transfer and flat areas, but a bulky revolving mangle is better because you can pull on the fabric as it feeds to make it flat. Use a pressing cloth to protect surfaces.

Notions: Any of the many sewing notions counters or catalogs will show wonderful things to use. Pin cushions, thread holder racks, bias tape makers, magnifiers, and more. Keep up on these for good new ideas. Also, see Sources of Supply.

Making Patchwork Squares

With graph paper in hand, Claudia and I searched for suitable traditional pieced block patterns and sketched little drawings about 1½″ square on the graph paper to see how they were assembled. Use your own favorites, or use some or all of the ones shown for Hattie's Birthday Quilt.

Next, determine the size design square or pieced block you plan to use. We chose an 8″ square. To do this decide what size you want the finished quilt to be, about how many units you want to include, and the size of spacers and border. Hattie's quilt is a single bed size (see How to Make Hattie's Birthday Quilt for specific dimensions). Use a ruler, calculator, and graph paper to lay out the width, length, and number of squares on the quilt (see Chapter 3).

The 8″ square we decided on required 35 units to fill the quilt, five across and seven high. Some traditional patterns we found needed to be adapted to this size, and some we changed to suit the album quilt needs. A few we invented (Fig. 7–6).

Traditional Piecework

Traditional squares fall into certain design patterns of geometric shapes. In the earliest known, the square is divided into quarters (four equal squares). Three patterns used on Hattie's quilt fall into this category. In "Windmill," the quarters are divided into triangles. In "King's X" the quarters are triangled and then split. "Star" is made up of 8 parallelograms, 4 squares and 4 triangles (Fig. 7-7).

Simple geometric shapes are used because of their satisfying design, and also because joining straight seams is the easiest way to sew. Curved seams and angled intersections are more difficult. The "Star" pattern requires pivoting on angled corners instead of stitching straight across: some quilters like such challenges.

"Nine Patch" divides the square into three and three again, resulting in nine squares (Fig. 7–7). This allows more versatility than quartering, and is still easy to make. Further subdividing some or all of the nine squares into rectangles gives great latitude for design. Hattie's quilt shows nine or ten variations. "Shoo Fly" is "Nine Patch" with the corners divided into triangles, "Bear's Paw" and "Maple Leaf" are similar, with four divided sections.

Many traditional squares are made in strips. "Amish Square" divides the square in half diagonally. One of these triangles is divided into four strips, each 1½″ wide. "Log Cabin" starts with a square and adds increasingly longer inch-wide strips (Fig. 7–7). "Album Block" is made of almost 2″-wide squares or strips, sewn into longer strips on the diagonal.

Fig. 7–7 Hattie's quilt contains many traditional pieced-block patterns, including a "Nine Patch" variation (upper left), "Album Block" (middle right), "Log Cabin" variation (lower left), and "Star" (lower right).

"Sail Boat," "Christmas Tree," "Cat," and "Hattie's Hat" are all assembled from squares and triangles. Each is symmetrical, with one side mirroring the other. The smallest pieces are assembled first. These small units are then assembled into strips, and the strips sewn together so the last seams are long and straight. Look for patterns that can be made this way.

Several patterns, especially "Grandmother's Fan" and "Fruit Basket," require that some pieces be appliquéd instead of pieced with seams. These curved pieces could be pieced, as in "Lafayette's Orange Peel," but it's more difficult.

Designing Patchwork

To make your own designs, begin by drawing a square the size you want to use on graph paper. Use a ruler, T-square, or triangle, to divide the square into halves, thirds, or other various straight or curved shapes.

For "Hattie's Hat" pattern I made several sketches of little girls, and finally settled on one wearing a hat because of its nice straight lines. I squared off the girl's face, hair, eyes, and mouth to make the fabric pieces geometric.

To design your own, sketch first and then use a T-square to make precise vertical and horizontal lines; use a triangle for angled lines. Use the compass or circle guide for drawing curved lines, but remember they are harder to join and may require appliquéing.

Changing Pattern Sizes

To change the scale of a pieced block pattern, draw the size block you want on graph paper. Analyze how the block is divided—quarters, thirds, halves? Divide your square in the same manner, using a ruler or your calculator. (An engineer's scale rule will measure in tenths to match calculator numbers.) Use your drafting tools to make an accurate new square. Compare angles to see that they are the same. Geometric patterns will be the easiest to change.

For other patterns, try using an opaque projector, photocopying, or photostating to make a different size. Many standard patterns are shown in books and magazines in various sizes, and are available as commercial templates.

Making Templates

After you've made an accurate, full-sized pattern on graph paper, test it. To do this, trace a copy on tracing paper, label each piece, and cut it into pieces along seam lines. These pieces (or thicker ones made by tracing them on cardboard or clear plastic) are called templates. These templates have no seam allowances, which must be added before cutting out fabric pieces.

The line you trace on fabric around the template is the stitching line. You must sew on this line to keep the pattern accurate. Unless you are British. Recently, I was busily stitching along my drawn lines on Hattie's quilt blocks while visiting friends in England. After comparing notes, we discovered that they sew the fabric over a paper or plastic template (Fig. 7–8). They whip stitch the adjoining edges, and then remove the template. In some antique pieced quilts, the newspaper templates remained in place, allowing accurate dating of the quilt.

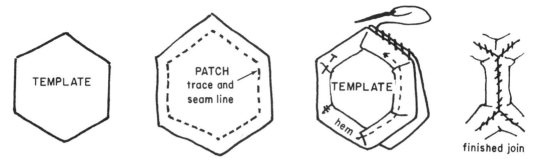

Fig. 7–8 The British method of hand-sewing pieced blocks: trace template on patch with seam allowance; fold hem over template, and pin or baste; then overcast stitches on edges to join patches. At right is the finished seam joining (from back).

This template technique works best on complex small designs like "Hexagon," "Star," or "Flower." It is possible to do this method by sewing machine if you are very accurate, but more bother than it is worth.

For either method, trace the template piece on selected fabric colors, always remembering to add seam allowances of ¼" or more. Trace your pieces with the grain of the fabric whenever possible. Assemble the blocks in the most logical fashion into small units or strips, and then into the whole block. If your newly designed block is too difficult to assemble, redesign it.

Cutting Blocks

If you find it hard to remember to add seam allowances, make patterns from the templates with ¼" or more seam allowances added. Pin them on or trace around them. Then trace a stitching line on the fabric pieces. You can also make or buy window templates. This frame-like template has a cutout center the shape of the pattern piece, and an outer edge the shape of the added seam allowance. Made window templates of plastic or sturdy cardboard because they are fragile.

To cut out fabric pieces, use any of the listed cutting tools that work for you, including the paper cutter.

Assembling Squares

Lay cutout fabric pieces in pieced block patterns to see if you like the colors. Claudia chose seven colors, ranging from rose and peach, to green and blue, with brown and dark green. Two are plain light colors for signatures, three are medium prints, and two are dark prints for contrast. These are fairly standard for patchwork quilts.

You can assemble each block as you cut it out, or cut out all the pieces and then stitch. If you cut them all first, you'll need some way to keep track of them until assembly. I stacked the pieces in horizontal rows, or in the order that they are assembled (Fig. 7–9). I tailor tacked them together, and attached an adhesive label with a little diagram.

Blocks can be machine or hand-sewn. Hattie's quilt is a mixture (I can hear the purists gasping out there!). I used machine-sewing for speed and hand-sewing for portability, tucking the stacks of blocks into a plastic bag for traveling. The stitches are tiny

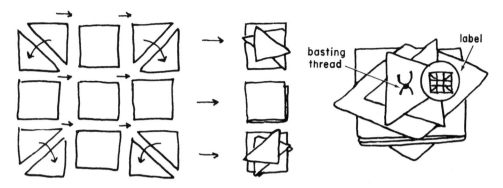

Fig. 7–9 Stack block pieces in same order they will be stitched. Baste together and label, with a sketch of the assembled block.

enough so it's hard to tell one from the other on the finished quilt.

Signing Squares

The earliest friendship quilt blocks were usually signed before piecing, allowing the quilt designer to place them where she chose (and to discard patches with ink blobs on them). Embroidered patches may well have been sewn after the pieced blocks were assembled, because the small pieces would not fit into hoops. Certainly, machine-embroidered blocks will need to be assembled first, or signed on fabric and then cut out.

Hattie's Birthday Quilt is traditional in most aspects, except this one: To sign the blocks, I traced signatures on tracing paper, pinned them in place, stretched the block in a hoop, and used free-motion machine-sewing to duplicate signatures. Furthermore, since most of the "friends" are Hattie's mother's—and Hattie's are yet to come, most of the signatures will be added over her lifetime to the finished quilt.

To do this, the quilt block will be stretched in a machine embroidery hoop, the tissue paper name pinned on, and free-motion machine-stitched in place. The bobbin thread should match the quilt backing. Yes, the stitching may show, but it helps quilt the layers.

Hattie's Birthday Quilt

QUILT PROFILE

OCCASION: Hattie Stroud's first birthday

GROUP: Family friends' signatures are on the quilt; Hattie's future friends' signatures will be added throughout her lifetime (a friendship quilt in the making)

QUILT DESIGNERS: Claudia Hall Stroud (mother) and Carolyn Vosburg Hall (grandmother)

ORGANIZATION: Claudia sent notes to friends requesting their signatures. I made blocks and machine-stitched the signatures.

THEME: A traditional 1840s-style friendship quilt.

TECHNIQUE: Traditional and original designs assembled by machine and hand, featuring free-motion machine-embroidered names

TIME: Begun in mid-summer of 1986, nearing completion by Hattie's birthday on October 20

SIZE: 60" × 80½"

BLOCK SIZE: 8" squares

LAYOUT: 35 blocks, 5 horizontal and 7 vertical; 2¼" sashing; 5½" borders

COLORS: Main color is dark green paisley print, with blocks in combinations of taupe, peach, dusty pink print, soft blue print, soft green print, and dark brown print.

YARDAGE TOTAL: 9¼ yards of 45" fabric

FILLER: Bonded polyester batting

QUILTING METHOD: Hand-quilted with a 24" wooden hoop

DISPLAY: Displayed on the guest bed

MATERIALS

(Buy extra fabric for safety margin)

Design patches: ½ yard each of peach, pink, taupe, green, blue, brown, and the main green	3½ yards
Border, spacers, backing and design patches	5¾ yards
two strips, 31" × 81½", for backing	
two strips, 6½" × 70½", for side borders	
two strips, 6½" × 61", top and bottom borders	
four strips, 3¼" × 70½", for vertical sashing	
thirty strips, 3¼" × 9", cut *lengthwise*	
Total	9¼ yards

Other supplies: bonded polyester quilting batt; dark green quilting thread or mercerized sewing thread (waxed) for quilting; tan thread for piecing squares, dark brown machine embroidery thread for signatures; 12" machine embroidery hoop, and 24" quilting hoop for hand quilting

Drafting supplies: graph paper, template cardboard, measuring and guide tools, markers, and cutters

PROCEDURE

Making Pieced Blocks

Generally, pattern pieces give the pattern name. Follow alphabetical order to assemble the blocks.

1. Trace or photocopy pattern pieces in Figures 7–10 through 7–12, or make your own designs. Trace each piece onto tracing paper, then onto heavier paper for templates. Transfer markings. (Templates have no seam allowances, so you may wish to make additional patterns with ¼" seam allowances.) Commercial plastic templates are cut like frames, so you trace inside the frame for the stitching line and outside for the cutting line. If you make your own template frames, use sturdy material since they are only ¼" wide.

2. Lay out the pattern with room for ¼" seam allowances on fabric, keeping with the grain of the fabric.

3. Trace around the template for stitching line. Add seam allowance.

4. Cut out the pieces and lay patches for each block in order to be assembled.

The "Nine Patch" Blocks

1. To make the basic "Nine Patch" and its related family of blocks, stack pieces in order from upper left across to lower right (see Fig. 7–9). Paper clip or pin through blocks, and stick on a diagram label so you won't forget how it assembles.

2. Starting at the upper left, match the drawn seam lines of the first two blocks. Place pins at the corners to align them, and hand or machine stitch on the drawn seam lines.

3. Align the third piece with the second, and stitch. This completes a row of three across. Repeat for each horizontal row. Press the seams to one side on each row.

4. Align the drawn stitching lines on the top and center rows. Pin the seams to align and stitch. Repeat for the bottom row. Check by eye and measure to see if the block is sewn accurately. If so, press the completed block. If not, take out the offending seams and restitch.

"Nine Patch" variations include "Shoo Fly," "Bear's Paw," "Maple Leaf," "Butterfly," "Box Kite," "Fish," "Eighteen Patch," and "Nine Patch Plus Four" patterns. They are all "Nine Patch" family members, with some squares divided into triangles (Fig. 7–10). To make any one of them, assemble the adjacent triangles into blocks (appliqué the "Maple Leaf" stem). Then proceed through the 4 steps above.

"Windmill" or "Whirlwind" Patch

1. Align and stitch the A patches (Fig. 7–10) together to make larger triangles.

2. Align and sew the assembled A patches to the B patches, keeping them in the right order.

3. Align the assembled upper left square with the upper right and stitch. Press. Repeat for the lower two squares.

4. Align the seams and corners of the two rows of blocks and sew. Press.

"Amish Square"

1. Align strip B to large triangle A and sew (Fig. 7–10).

2. Align C to B and stitch, D to C and

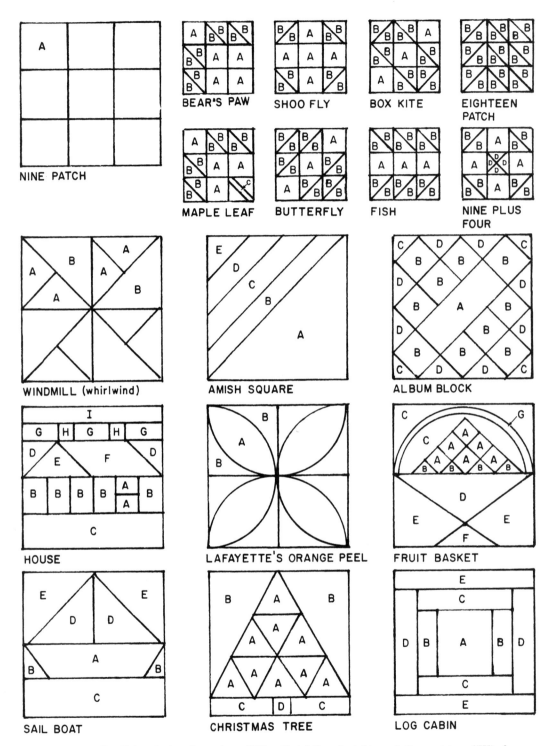

Fig. 7–10 Traditional pieced patches: "Nine Patch" and eight variations at top; "Windmill," "Amish Square," "Album Block," "House," "Lafayette's Orange Peel," "Fruit Basket," "Sail Boat," "Christmas Tree," and "Log Cabin." Assemble all blocks in alphabetical order.

stitch, and E to D and stitch. Press the completed block.

3. Glue-baste a heart patch (cut with no seam allowances) on the large triangle and machine appliqué in place (see Fig. 7–13). Or straight topstitch the heart in place and overlay with decorative machine stitching. For hand sewing, press a ¼″ hem all around the heart and pin in place. Hand sew with hidden stitches.

"Log Cabin"

1. Begin with the center square (Fig. 7–10). Align one 4″ B piece to the edge and sew. Align a second B to the opposite edge and sew. Press by iron or finger-press seams to the outer edge as you go.

2. Align a 6″ C piece to the top edge of A and B. Align and sew a second C piece to the bottom edge.

3. Align a D piece to the right side of the assembled unit and sew. Make sure the inner pieces are accurate widths. Repeat with a second D piece on the left edge.

4. Align an 8″ E piece to the top and sew. Align an E piece to the bottom and sew. Press the completed square.

"Album Block"

1. Join Bs to each end of A (Fig. 7–10). Join C triangles to ends of Bs. This completes the longest center diagonal strip.

2. Join three Bs in a row. Join end Bs to Ds. Repeat to make two diagonal strips.

3. Join D on each end of a B. Repeat for two diagonal strips.

4. Beginning in one corner, join C to D/B/D row, this to D/B/B/B/D row, this to center D/B/A/B/D row. Complete square in reverse order. Press.

"House"

1. Join A pieces for window (Fig. 7–10).

2. Join center row of five B pieces, including A in the fifth spot.

3. Join ground C to B row.

4. Join D to E, E to F, and F to D. Join this completed row to B row.

5. Join G to H, H to G, G to H, and H to G. Join this row to top of roof/sky unit.

6. Join I to the top of the unit. Press.

"Lafayette's Orange Peel"

1. Join curved A piece to curved B (Fig. 7–10). Join B to opposite side of A. Press flat. Repeat 4 times.

2. Join top two completed squares into a row. Repeat. Join the two rows at the seams and corners. Press flat.

"Sail Boat"

1. Join boat A to B at one end (Fig. 7–10). Join B to other end.

2. Join A/B row to water C.

3. Join sail D to D. Join D to E at each side.

4. Join completed row E/D/D/E to A/B. Press.

"Christmas Tree"

1. Join A (point up) to A (point down), add A (point up), add A (point down), add A (point up) to complete the bottom row of the tree (Fig. 7–10).

2. For the next row, join a center A (point down) to two side As (points up).

3. Join first row (five As) to second row (three As). Add A (point up) on top to complete tree triangle.

4. Join B triangles to A tree on each side.

5. Assemble row C/D/C, and sew to A. Press.

"Fruit Basket"

1. Join three As and one B in a row. Join two As and one B. Join one A and one B. Join three A/B to two A/B to AB. Hem the right angle corner.

2. Pin or glue-baste assembled A/B piece on C (5″ × 9″ background). Top-stitch.

3. Hem the basket handle G and pin or glue baste on C. Topstitch in place.

4. Align and sew D to one E. Align and sew the other E to F. Align D/E to E/F at the seam and corners and sew straight across.

5. Align D to C and stitch, covering the raw edges of As and Bs.

"Grandmother's Fan"

1. Join A to A five times to make the fan (Fig. 7–11). Press the fan, and press a ¼″ hem along the top edge.

2. Pin or glue-baste the fan in place on B (9″-square background). Top-stitch by machine or fasten with hidden hand-stitching. Embellish with decorative stitching to cover machine topstitching, if you wish.

3. Press a hem in C. Pin or glue-baste over the raw edges of fan A and topstitch to complete the block.

"King's X"

1. Keep pieces in order (Fig. 7–11). (I didn't, you might notice on one square.) In the upper left square, join A to B, and A to B. Join A to A to complete square. Repeat four times.

2. Join the upper left A/B to upper right A/B. Repeat for the bottom two squares.

3. Join the top row to the bottom, matching seams and corners.

"Hattie's Hat"

1. Hem three sides of eyes A and all sides of mouth B (Fig. 7–11). Glue-baste in place on face C and machine-appliqué. Or, add no seam allowances and glue-baste A and B to C, and machine-appliqué.

2. Join hair D to face C on each side. Join bangs E to top of face A, stitching over unhemmed top of eyes A. Join F to each side of D/E to complete row.

3. Join row G to F/E/F row.

4. Join hat band H to hat top I. Join J to each side to complete row.

5. Join top row J/H/I/J to hat band G to complete square.

"Cat"

1. Join nose, eye, and cheek As together (Fig. 7–12). Join six As to B.

2. Join B/A unit to C on each side to complete center row.

3. Join D to E. Join second E to D. Align and join Es, or join Es at nose. Join E/D/E row to C/A/A/A/C row.

4. Join ears F to G on each side. Join F/G/F to C/B/C.

5. Join H to E/D/E row.

6. Join I row to each side to complete square. Press.

7. Glue baste eye J to eye A. Satin-stitch in place. Repeat for each eye. Add stitched whiskers if you wish.

"Star"

I saved the most difficult—"Star" and "Flower"—for last (Fig. 7–12) To make "Star" easier to machine sew, split the C pieces and make this patch in two sections with seam allowances. To make this pattern the standard way, follow these directions:

1. Join A to A. Stitch A to B, pivot on B, and sew to second A. Repeat three more times.

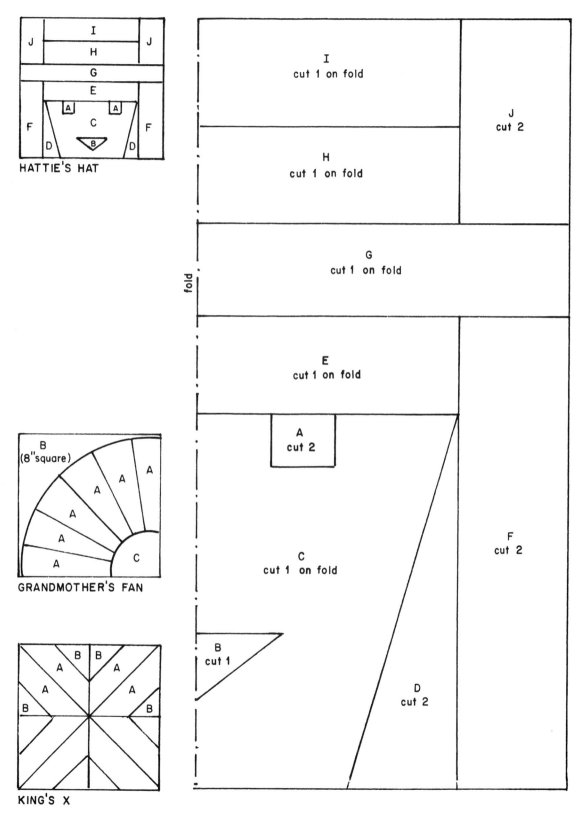

Fig. 7–11 "Hattie's Hat" (full-size pattern), "Grandmother's Fan" and "King's X" diagrams. Assemble in alphabetical order.

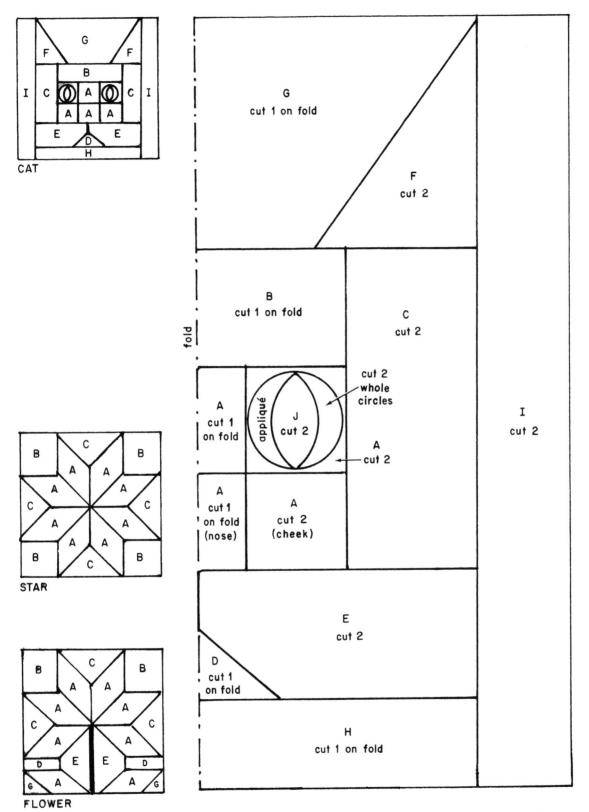

Fig. 7-12 Full-size pattern for "Cat." "Star" and "Flower" piecing diagrams. Assemble in alphabetical order. scale.

2. Join top left A/B/A to top right A/B/A. Repeat for lower left and right.

3. Join top row A/B/A/A/B/A to lower row.

4. Join C to A. At the seam, pivot on C and sew to second A. Repeat four times to finish the block. Check the square to see if it is flat. If not, rip out and restitch seams, then press.

"Flower"

1. Hem stem F and glue-baste or pin to E (Fig. 7–12). Topstitch.

2. Assemble the top of the flower A/B/A/C/A/B/A, following the first two steps above for making the top half of "Star."

3. For bottom half, sew C to A to D. Repeat.

4. Join C/A/D to one side of E by joining A to E up to the seam line, pivot on E and sew D to E. Repeat to join the second C/A/D to the other side.

5. Join leaf A to G. Repeat.

6. Join leaf A/G to E/D by sewing A to E up to seam line, pivoting on A and sewing A to D.

Fig. 7–13 Names were free-motion machine stitched through a signed paper signature for accuracy. The cat's whiskers were added at the same time.

7. Align C/A/E/A/C to flower A/A and sew, pivoting on the corners to complete the block.

Stitching Signatures

To free-machine embroider, use the darning setting, darning spring, or darning foot, or loosen the pressure foot, whichever you are accustomed to on your machine.

1. Stretch and align the block in a machine embroidery hoop: make sure it is perfectly straight.

2. Trace the signature onto tracing paper and pin it to the square securing in two places.

3. Trace the signature with tiny machine stitches. Guide by moving your hands slowly but firmly, and run the machine at a moderate to quick speed. Tear away the paper and clip threads.

To hand embroider, use cotton or silk embroidery floss. Use a tiny back-stitch to make a smooth line for the signature. It is easier to embroider before assembling the quilt, but you can add signatures later, in the same manner.

Assembling Blocks, Spacers, and Borders

1. Check to see if all blocks lie flat and have correct seam allowances. If not, use an 8″ template to redraw accurate seam lines around the perimeter of the blocks. Use a different color of wax pencil if necessary to distinguish lines.

2. To make a horizontal row, align and sew spacers to the right sides of four blocks. Join left sides of blocks (including fifth block, excluding the opposite end block) to spacers to complete the row. Repeat for all seven rows.

3. Join all rows but one to horizontal spacer strip. Join each row to the next row spacer to complete block section.

4. Join the side borders to the block section.

5. Join the top and bottom borders to the block to complete the quilt face.

See Chapter 12 for quilting layers and finishing the quilt. Hattie's Birthday Quilt was made like a comforter, with finished edges then hand-quilted in a 24″ quilting hoop in front of the TV on winter nights.

Chapter 8

Hand and Machine Appliqué
The Artists' Quilt

Remember when you cut and pasted happily as a child, making colored paper shapes to create bolder scenes than crayons could manage? Appliqué, with fabric patches like paper cutouts, has this same directness. It works up fast and looks delightful. This chapter tells how to join the fun by appliquéing in several ways by hand and machine.

Appliqué's easy design gives friends a way to make satisfying friendship quilt squares, no matter what their artistic or needlework skills. You can further ensure success by encouraging everyone to proceed only so far as they feel comfortable, then offer to finish for them. This way they can stop with a sketch, send back a cutout design, or sew a finished appliqué patch themselves. As a result, you get the friend's personal touch, and your sewing standards.

On most friendship quilts, we sent out a kit including a background square and a collection of five or six appliqué fabric swatches, each measuring about 6″ by 9″ or larger. We asked friends to follow the theme suggested and to make an appliqué block using backing to stabilize the square for machine-appliqué, or using the fabric square as is for hand appliqué, or leav-

ing the sewing to us if they chose. Usually, one of these choices meshed with their skills.

Never underestimate your friends. On most squares returned, people showed instinctive good sense about using the bold shapes that work best with appliqué. And, when they found it difficult to cut narrow strips and complicated shapes, they avoided them. Their designs grew out of the nature and limitations of the materials, as good designs will.

About five people per quilt asked for sewing help. Most other quilt designers report a similar number. Like most quilt designers, I enjoy finishing additional squares, and usually do them all the same day. It makes the friends I help feel wanted, and it gives me a chance to add outline colors, and change blocks enough to help balance the overall quilt design.

Making the Artists' Quilt

Appliquéd flowers seemed a perfect theme for my friends in The Birmingham Society of Women Painters. So many of them paint flowers exquisitely. Surprise. Some didn't like my theme because they don't like being

Fig. 8–1 The Artists' Quilt has several elements in its layout: a large central square with a frame; twelve colorful appliquéd flowers on alternating white-and-navy squares with a frame; added strips to make the quilt rectangular; and a border.

Amy's
Wedding
Quilt

The Kids' Quilt

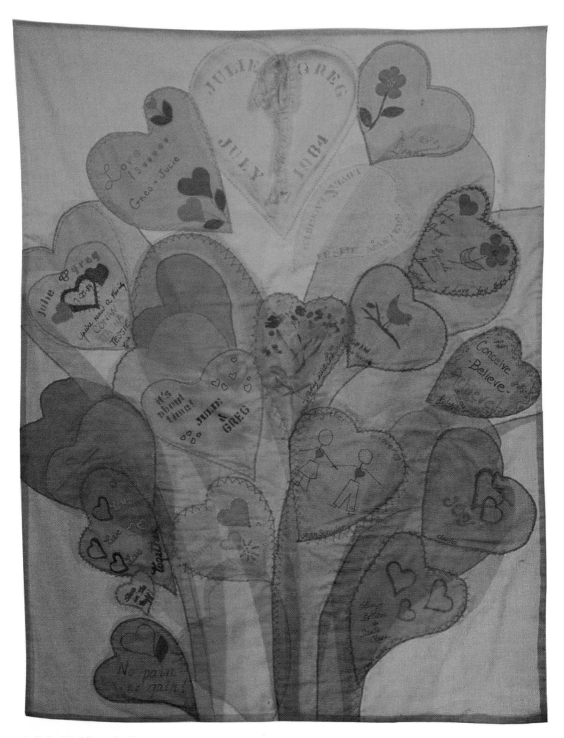

Julie's Wedding Quilt

Mary's Birthday Quilt

Carolyn's
"SS Friendship" Quilt

Gerald Ford's
Bicentennial Quilt

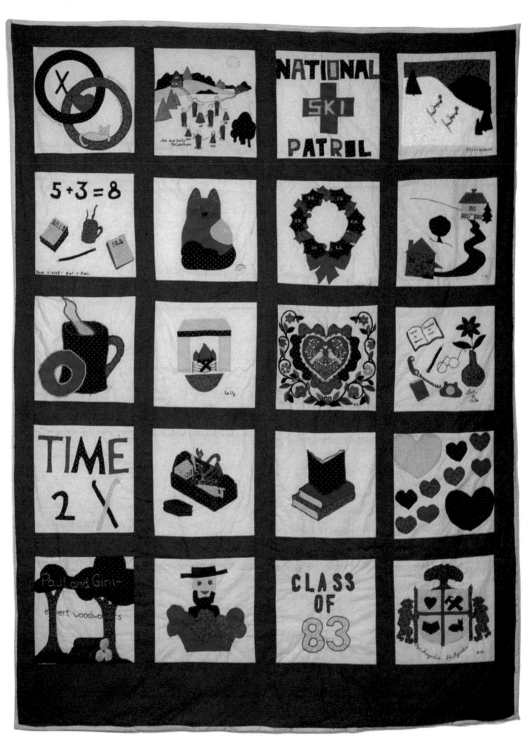

Gini's Wedding Quilt

Colleen's Wedding Quilt

The Birmingham Bicentennial Quilt

categorized as "lady flower painters." (It does help to find out how contributors feel about your request.) Most of my friends returned drawings or paintings for me to interpret in appliqué, rather than stitch blocks themselves. These painters doubted that their stitchery would do justice to their drawings, so they accepted my offer to translate them into fabric. Not all did so, though. Dorothy Delehanty made a three-dimensional stuffed flower and butterfly, Fran Waring used both the face and reverse sides of a print fabric for subtle color shading on her tulip, and Leslie used favorite rainbow colors to outline her bright-hued flower (see Fig. 8-1).

Organization for this quilt varied from the usual means of mailing kits in several ways. Every variation caused problems, but that's what creativity is all about — solving problems, finding out what will work and what won't.

I'd made so many quilts for others, I decided it was my turn. Asking for blocks for oneself changes dynamics. People don't respond as readily. Yet women made those earliest friendship quilts for themselves. How did they do it?

They worked out trades. Women have exchanged quilt blocks for so many generations that niceties have developed: don't ask for too much, give something in return, thank the block-maker, and more. (Chapter 2 gives more details.) My painter friends didn't want blocks in return, so I offered them the chance to appear in this book and in our annual painting exhibition as part of the quilt. Even so, the main reason they made blocks for me is that they are generous friends of long standing.

Second problem: I had no decisive deadline. Yes, I mentioned a date, but it didn't involve a party or get-together. Finally, as the exhibition deadline grew closer — a reality all artists understand — their flowers bloomed.

As if I hadn't deviated enough, at first I requested cutout flowers of any shape about 12" across. I planned to appliqué them in a random, pleasing arrangement across the quilt face. Without adequate instructions, the artists found it hard to make designs befitting their standards. I changed format, offering white or navy 13" background squares to frame each flower separately. I appliquéd the first few finished flowers in place, so everyone could see how good they looked. This brought more flowers.

By deadline, twelve flowers had come back, not quite enough for the checkerboard quilt I had in mind. I began to lay them out in my studio, when suddenly I could see that a big 24" square in the center would do wonders. Too much contrast existed between the navy and white squares. A large, mid-range colored square would pull it all together.

I spread, folded, tucked, and arranged various-colored swatches of fabric until an overall design began to emerge. I used a navy-and-white tiny print to frame the flower blocks. Periwinkle-purple fabric bordered the garden cheerfully. But one part was missing, a top and bottom strip to make the quilt rectangular. I must have tried fourteen fabrics before I found a Malaysian batik piece I'd saved because it never went with anything. At last, it found the perfect home.

All the hassle and travail on this quilt were worth the effort. It turned out to be a strong, individual quilt, and was requested for two upcoming quilt shows.

Planning an Appliquéd Quilt

Appliqué can be done in many ways, as you've seen from examples in this book. Most often, you will be sending out kits and directions for appliqué, with strict instructions not to add other materials. This results in a controlled style, such as Peter's Wedding Quilt.

To create a playful quilt, you will probably send out kits and request a general friendship theme, giving wide latitude with technique for adding other trims, colors, ribbons or fabrics as friends wish. Some participants will appliqué as you expect, but some will piece, or gather, or stuff, glue, paint, or whatever with their fabrics. These everything-goes quilts are harder to arrange but more inventive and often funny. Lori's Wedding Quilt and the Minister's Retirement Quilt are this type.

For something as technically accurate as the Artists' Quilt, you'll need tighter control. You can specify the theme, suggest a color range, and request drawings only, saying that you plan to appliqué them yourself, unless your friends are all skilled stitchers.

For scenic appliqué, such as the Birmingham Bicentennial Quilt, send a kit or suggest a color range, and send a photograph or drawing of the scene you want portrayed (Fig. 8–2). Describe what you want accomplished. Have meetings to choose colors, pass on drawings for squares, and assist each other if necessary. See Chapter 13 for details on this quilt.

Fig. 8–2 A square from the Birmingham Bicentennial Quilt; squares are scenes of the town, done in hand and machine appliqué, adapted from drawings and photographs.

Drawing for Appliqué

The most successful, easiest-to-sew appliqués have large color areas with few or no small pieces, elaborate shapes, or narrow strips. At this stage the design may lack punch, but colorful satin-stitching can outline shapes, delineate interior details, or ramble about the design as needed for accent. The combination of fabric shapes and colorful outlines creates good appliqués.

Hand-sewn appliqués are nearly always hemmed along the edges to give a finished look and keep them from fray-

114

ing. This requires keeping shapes simple. Machine-appliqué covers the raw edge and does not require seam allowances; you can use more elaborate shapes.

Ask friends who send drawings to think in large solid areas, without subtle shading. Suggest they simplify the forms (discussion on doing this appears in Chapter 4). Also ask for full-

Fig. 8–3 Leslie Masters Villani used rainbow colors for her flower (at left, on white). Garden lilies in bloom allowed me to draw directly from the flowers for my appliquéd square (top right).

115

sized drawings. Scaling up is a pain, but it's described in Chapter 7.

Follow these steps to make a drawing into an appliqué:

1. Lay tracing paper over the drawing (or photograph) and trace the outline of each area. If one shape (a face, for example) shades from light to dark, determine where the shading divides and draw a line to separate the two areas. Your aim is to simplify the drawing, and reduce it to flat color areas. If the shapes are complicated, see where you can simplify them without losing the character of the design. To check the success of your design, color the spaces with colored pencils, or cut them out in colored paper to see how it looks. Make any necessary changes. When you have the design the way you want it, make an accurate tracing on tracing paper.

2. Iron the fabric to be used for appliqué pieces. Wrinkles will distort shapes.

3. To trace pattern pieces, use one of these two methods: (1) Lay the traced patterns on a light box, window, or glass-topped table, with the ironed fabric over the pattern, and trace the pattern pieces with tailor's chalk if you add seam allowances, light pencil if not; or (2) if you prefer, make two tracings and cut one out for patterns to trace around. For machine appliqué, you can trace and cut on the outline, adding a ¼" seam allowance where one piece overlaps another. For hand appliqué and the second type of machine appliqué, add at least ¼" seam allowances around every piece, including where pieces meet each other.

4. Cut out all the fabric pieces.

5. Plan to assemble the appliqué from the "outside" or "bottom" inward or upward. For example, the outside petals of a flower would be placed and sewn first (Fig. 8–4). Overlapping petals come next. The center piece that overlaps them all comes last. It's difficult or impossible to tuck a piece under one already sewn down, so be sure to plan ahead.

6. Lay the pieces on the background in order, and adjust the tracing paper pattern over them to check for accuracy of placement. Or, you can do this in reverse. Place the topmost piece on the underside of the tracing paper pattern and pin it in place. Keep adding pieces until the design is completed. Then place the whole design with the tracing paper on the background.

The next step is to stitch your design to the background. Pieces without seam allowances are affixed and sewn one way, pieces with seam allowances another. These methods follow.

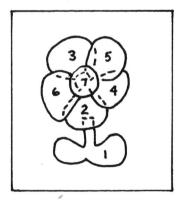

Fig. 8–4 Analyze your drawing for the most logical sequence of overlapping appliqué pieces. Then number them, as here (dashed lines are "underneath" edges).

116

Machine Appliqué

Machine appliqué makes the quickest, most wonderful quilt squares — or it leads to frustration and saying all those words you don't like people to know you know. These four criteria make machine appliqué work best:

1. The background fabric is firmly woven and stable enough so it does not stretch or pucker;
2. Appliqué pieces are firmly woven and well anchored;
3. Fabric appliqués are dense enough to avoid visible overlaps and glue baste marks;
4. The machine embroidery hoop fits your square properly.

Results will also depend greatly on your sewing machine. Jackie Dodson says the ten-year-old mid-line Bernina (830) makes the best satin stitch. My older Singer Genie portable sews a nice line. My Kenmore makes a wonderful feather stitch, but it can be fractious on satin stitches. Sewing machine models change all the time, so it's hard to recommend the best one.

If you have a good zigzag machine, you can set it to do appliqué, but you must be sure to keep your machine manual ready to consult. Spend some time with your machine to develop a good satin-stitch before making an appliqué quilt.

Needles

Use a sharp new needle, the smallest possible for the thread you have chosen. Ballpoint needles, designed for synthetics, push the fabric fibers apart, rather than piercing them. Regular needles are sharp enough to pierce cottons cleanly. Keep a good supply of various types and sizes of needles of the right brand for your machine. Buy assorted sizes in case you need a bigger threading hole.

Threads

Many different threads, including regular sewing thread, work fine for appliqué. Special machine-embroidery threads are even better. The regular Mercerized cotton, or cotton-coated polyester-core sewing threads come in a wide variety of colors and on large cones as well. Silk and rayon threads have a beautiful sheen; however, some of these shiny threads may slide off the spool, tangle, or break readily.

My favorite is a double-weight cotton machine-embroidery thread, with a soft twist so it spreads out to fill in the satin stitching. Sometimes I use two regular sewing threads on top for quicker buildup. I'm now trying some of the stretchy threads designed for softer stitching on sergers, and they seem to work well.

If stores near you do not stock machine-embroidery threads, you can order them by mail (see Sources of Supply).

Machine Settings

You can adjust your machine several ways to alter the stitch.

Stitch Length: Use the stitches-per-inch lever or dial to activate the feed dogs, those little jaggers that come up and down in the needle plate to move the fabric forward or back. This controls stitch length.

Stitch Width: Use the sideway swing of the needle to make wide stitches.

Using the control lever, you can make these stitches vary from the tiniest fraction wide to more than ¼" on some models. To satin stitch, experiment with various combinations of stitch length and width. The shorter the stitches, the more solid the satin stitch. The wider the width, the wider the satin stitch.

Thread Tension: Change the tension control (with plus and minus on it) on the top thread to make looser or tighter stitches. On some machines you can also alter the bobbin tension so both form a looser stitch. Tight stitches pucker the background fabric, so tension control is all-important for appliqué.

Presser Foot Pressure: On some machines you can set the presser foot pressure manually. Others adjust automatically. I prefer to set this myself to ease the fabric under the presser foot more readily, or do free-motion sewing.

Presser Feet: All machines take different accessory feet for different kinds of stitching. The appliqué foot is wide enough for zigzag stitching, has a groove on the underside to clear a thick row of satin stitches, and may be clear plastic for better view. For free-motion satin stitching, the darning foot may work best and not catch on a thread pile.

Anatomy of a Satin Stitch

The strongest machine straight stitch forms when the top and bobbin threads meet evenly within the fabrics joined, and neither row pulls the other out of place. This is called a balanced stitch.

A satin stitch has different requirements. It must loop back and forth upon itself and cover solidly. An unbalanced stitch works best here (Fig. 8–5). To make the satin stitch, unbalance the machine tension setting by reducing the top thread tension. The top thread is pulled through the fabric and is visible on the back, preventing the bobbin thread from showing on the face. The top edge of the satin stitching looks neater, since all the twists where top and bobbin threads join occur on the back side. I use a really unbalanced stitch, partly because it takes far less bobbin thread.

On some machines you can reduce the tension on the top and bobbin threads for a doubly loose satin stitch. (Most machine-repair men imply your sewing machine will vaporize if you touch the bobbin setting.)

Practice making a good satin stitch in various widths and thicknesses. The thread you use will influence the stitch. Aim for the closest possible solid stitching that does not pile up under the presser foot and halt forward progress. You'll have to stop and remove these built-up lumps. Clip them from the back.

If you just can't set the stitch close enough, sew over the line a second time to fill in gaps. As a general rule,

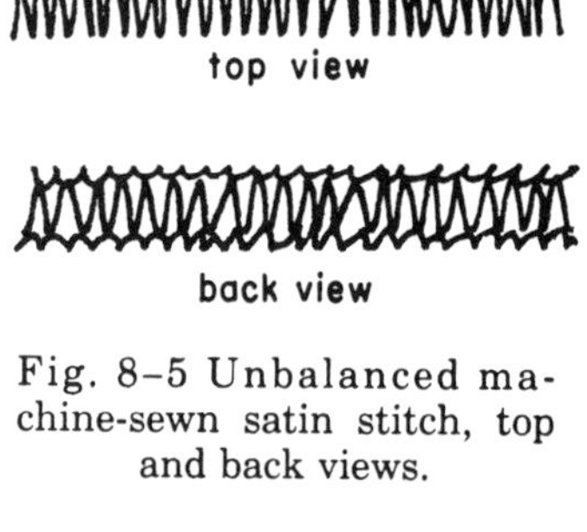

top view

back view

Fig. 8–5 Unbalanced machine-sewn satin stitch, top and back views.

sew less than full-width satin stitching, since the widest stitch will be apt to pull in and pucker the fabric.

Preparing the Appliqués

If friends have returned cutout designs for you to sew, use instructions marked CO. For appliqué pieces with seam allowances, use instructions marked SS for seams.

Placement (CO): Adjust the cutout appliqué pieces on the background fabric so they overlap a small amount where pieces join, if possible. This allows you to join edges of both pieces to the background with a single satin-stitch row. If this distorts the design, you will need to satin stitch around each piece separately.

Affixing: Use one of these six ways to affix the applied pieces to the background fabric.

1. (CO or SS) Glue fabric pieces in place with a new stick of a good brand of fabric glue-baste. Spread a thin layer around the edges of the appliqué piece, and press it onto the background fabric. (Be wary of old glue sticks. Glue comes off too thick, and will gunk up your sewing machine needle, or glue gobs will show through your fabric. Black mildew spots may form on old glue. Other than this, it's wonderful stuff.)

2. (CO or SS) Pin the pieces in place. Place fine tailor's pins at right angles to the stitch line at the edge. Use lots. It takes a "porcupine quill" row of pins to hold some pieces in place.

3. (CO or SS) If your fabric frays, coat the edges with "Fray-no-More," or use a glue stick.

4. (CO) For loosely woven fabric that you know will fray, use an iron-on backing or fusible lining material. A double-sided fuser such as Stitch Witchery allows you to both stabilize and affix the piece to the background. This backing does change the hand of the fabric, giving it a stiffer surface.

5. (CO or SS) For designs with small, shifting pieces, use clear tape and stick them in place. Later, sew over the tape with basting stitches, and then remove it along the perforated needle lines.

6. (CO or SS) Place your design on the background fabric loosely, or affixed in any of the previous ways *except* pinning. Lay the tracing paper pattern of the design over it; position the pattern and pin through the paper and patches to hold them in place. Do not place pins on the stitching line. You will be able to baste or satin stitch right through the tracing paper for a nice, flat appliqué. The paper will tear away along stitch lines, although you may need to tweeze a few bits out of the stitches, depending on the type of paper.

Stabilizing Background Fabric: Machine appliqué requires a firm, taut base fabric to counteract the pull of satin stitching. Accomplish this in one of several ways if your background fabric is not heavy enough:

1. Use scrap paper, typing paper, or newspaper, pinned on the back, during stitching. Remove it along stitching lines later. All of it will come off of basting stitches, but some will remain under the satin-stitched line. That's okay—it acts as support. In addition, the tracing paper overlay on top of the design acts to stabilize. You'll be sewing a paper sandwich.

2. Use a permanent fabric backing on the entire background fabric, such as sheeting or pre-shrunk broadcloth. Or use fusible iron-on backing all over or in appliqué spots. Trim around this backing after appliquéing if you wish.

3. Use a machine-embroidery hoop,

Fig. 8–6 Frieda Rubin's iris was machine basted with tiny straight stitches. Then, the extra fabric was trimmed away. The iris is now being satin stitched around each appliqué to cover the raw edges. See finished square in Fig. 8–1.

with or without one of the above backings. Your sewing machine and fabric will dictate how much of this preparation you will need to get good, flat results. On some machines you will need almost none and you can zoom right ahead.

Machine Basting: Machine basting improves machine appliqué, but does take extra time. Satin stitching will cover your basting stitches (Fig. 8–6). You can baste through the tissue paper overlay, and remove it before satin stitching, unless necessary design lines would be removed. If so, baste design lines and remove paper. Use one of these ways to baste.

1. Set your machine for a tiny satin stitch, and sew around the edge of each piece, shifting at each turn.

2. Set your machine for straight stitch, and reduce pressure on the presser foot. Free-motion machine baste the piece in place. This saves time and energy, since you don't need to shift in sewing around curves as you guide by hand.

3. Hand baste with running stitches.

Planning Outline Colors: Fabric patches provide colorful shapes, but the satin-stitched outline or other decorative appliqué stitching provides the accent. Use this chance to add threads in strong colors, elegant lines, and decorative touches. As a rule, for an unaccented shape, choose a related thread color in a darker or brighter shade for an outline. White or light outlines on light backgrounds don't show up well.

You need not outline each patch in its own color. Use contrasting colors, or choose one or two outline colors that will suit the entire design. I have a favorite warm brown I use for almost everything. On the Artists' Quilt, I used a dark green to outline a variety of different leaf colors, which gave a certain continuity from one patch to another.

Try various combinations of patches and thread colors on paper with colored pencils before beginning to stitch. This important choice of color makes an enormous difference in the results. Use your artist's eye and try some creative combinations. Study details of quilts shown in the color section to see what color combinations worked well.

Planning the Stitch Pattern: Examine your design to see where stitch lines begin and end. Plan to sew lines as continuously as possible, first completing background and edge outlines whose ends will be overlapped. Plan to sew all of the secondary color at once, then all of the primary or top color last.

Stitching Unhemmed Patches

1. Align the needle over the edge of the applied patch so the outside swing of the needle penetrates just past the edge of the fabric patch, and the inside swing bites into the patch the width of the satin stitch. The outline is functional, as well as decorative. It holds the patch in place, and must catch enough of the fabric patch to hold it securely. As you sew, keep in mind that the satin stitch is first an anchoring stitch, and secondly a decorative line.

2. Stitch at a comfortable speed, guiding the satin-stitched line around curves with care (Fig. 8–7). Be sure not to ruck up the patch. Lift the presser foot, and reposition as often as needed to turn corners and keep a smooth surface.

3. Use your hands, spread on each side of the stitching (even with a hoop) to carefully control progress (Fig. 8–8). Keep a sensitive touch so you can help the machine along, and avoid thread pile-ups under the presser foot.

4. Make overlap corners to avoid openings in the stitch line on square corners. To do this, stop the needle on the outside of a corner to be turned (Fig. 8–7B). Pivot the fabric on the needle, and begin to sew, overlapping the previous stitches (Fig. 8–7C).

5. If any lines are not as solid as you like, stitch over them a second time. Keep your seam ripper handy to re-

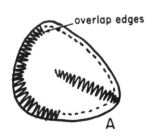 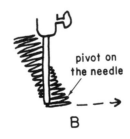 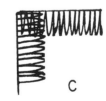

Fig. 8–7 Machine satin stitching. A. Satin stitches anchor the piece and emphasize outlines, too. Stitches must overlap edges completely. B. Pivot on needle to overlap satin stitches on corners to avoid gaps in the line. C. Overlap stitches and continue along new edge.

121

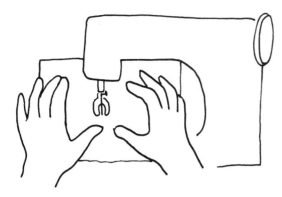

Fig. 8–8 Use your hands like a hoop to firmly and surely guide the fabric under the needle.

move poor stitching. You are drawing with your sewing machine, and want artistic results.

6. Don't bother to clip threads as you sew, but move to the next stitching area. Clip only those threads that catch on the presser foot. This saves having to pull the top and bottom threads out and to one side before beginning to sew. When you've finished one color, clip all the thread ends, front and back. A medium-width satin stitch is not apt to fray, but if you wish, pull top threads through to the back and tie before clipping.

7. Add the next color, overlapping the ends of the first color. Clip threads as described. Add any additional stitchery needed. Tear off any removable backing, or trim any permanent backing seam allowances you don't want.

Stitching Patches with Seam Allowances

The most complex appliqués can be made by basting the fabric in place on the seam line, trimming the seam allowances, and top stitching the result. Flowers on the Artists' Quilt were made by this technique.

1. Begin with a *stabilized* background fabric. Cut out designs with a ½″ seam allowance or more. If you use an overlay paper pattern, you need not trace outlines. Just cut a piece large enough to extend beyond the design outlines.

2. Lay pieces in place on the background fabric with upper colors overlapping lower colors. Or use this method: Lay the pieces on the back of the traced design pattern. Put the topmost color on the back of the traced design; for example, the center of a flower. Make sure the fabric extends beyond outlines of the pattern and pin this to the back of the paper pattern (Fig. 8–9, step 1). Then, add the next color patches — a row of petals surrounding the center. Finally, add the lowest pattern pieces — the outside ring of petals. Pin assembled pattern and patches in place on the background fabric.

3. Set your machine to a narrow, short zigzag. This stitch holds more firmly than a straight stitch. Baste around the outline of each color patch. (If you are handy, do free-motion basting, so the fabric won't have to be shifted.)

4. Tear off the tracing paper pattern. If accent lines will be lost, save those pattern pieces to repin in place later.

5. Use appliqué scissors, or very sharp sewing scissors, to trim away the seam allowances $\frac{1}{16}$″ outside each basting line (Fig. 8–9, step 5). Use extreme care not to cut the background fabric or the basting stitches. Keep your scissors at an angle and take short snips. This step may take a long time to trim one patch after another. Don't rush. Brush away frayed threads.

6. Satin stitch over the basting lines

122

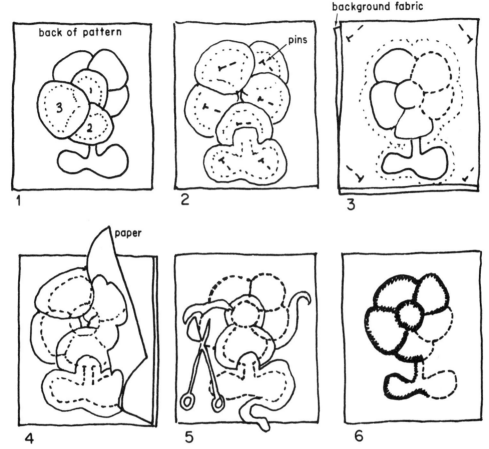

Fig. 8–9 Unhemmed machine appliqué. 1. On back of pattern, place topmost fabric piece with seam allowances extending beyond image lines. 2. Add fabric pieces until design is completely covered. Pin in place. 3. Position pinned pattern on background square. Machine baste lines. 4. Remove paper. 5. Trim away seam allowances to basting lines. 6. Satin stitch over all raw edges, covering basting stitches.

in the same manner as before (Fig. 8–9, step 6). Add detail lines and decorative stitching as needed.

Hemmed Appliqué by Hand

All hand appliqué, except for felt or other non-fray fabrics, requires a hem for a neat finished edge. Machine appliqué done with open decorative stitchery can benefit from a hemmed edge as well. A hem makes a neat fin-

ish on any seam not covered with stitching.

To make hemmed appliqué, follow these instructions:

1. Make a paper pattern. Trace the fabric over the pattern on a light source, or trace around a cutout pattern, using a removable marking (tailor's chalk). Add ¼" seam allowances around all edges of each appliqué piece (Fig. 8–11, step 1). (Some overlap and some will be hemmed.)

123

2. Cut out the fabric pieces.

3. Plan your design so you know which pieces will be overlapped by others. Plan to stitch the outermost or underneath piece first. You will not be able to tuck a later piece under one already sewn down.

4. Mark on each piece where hems occur and where underlaps occur. The hem will be turned under, the underlap will lie flat. Clip the seam allowance to the edge of the design where a hem changes to an underlap.

5. Finger or steam press hems in each piece. Clip inside curves almost to the seam line so the seam allowance will not pull (Fig. 8–11, step 2). On outside curves, make clips or notches to remove extra fabric. If you are using a flexible fabric, avoid clipping since it can lead to fraying. For a smooth round curve, run a gathering thread in the seam allowance, pull to shape, and press (Fig. 8–11, step 3). Hand baste if the hems won't stay pressed.

6. Place the undermost piece first, and pin in place. For hand-sewing, you may choose to sew each piece in place, one at a time. Add each successive piece, overlapping the first. Continue to build your design, adding pieces until it is completed.

7. To hand-sew, use sewing thread and make tiny hidden stitches at the edge to anchor the piece firmly to the background fabric (Fig. 8–11, step 4). Or use decorative hand embroidery stitches to attach (Fig. 8–11, step 5).

8. For machine appliqué, set your machine for a straight stitch, blind hem stitch, feather stitch, blanket stitch, or other decorative stitch, and topstitch the edges of each piece.

9. Old-time hand appliqué was often sewn with a blanket stitch that gave an

Fig. 8–10 Agnes Goodrich feather-stitched her figure by hand for Peter's Quilt, showing the delightful character of hand appliqué.

outline of "shading" stitches for charming effect. Try various stitches, and use what you like best.

Outline stitching need not always follow the appliqué shapes exactly. After you've anchored shapes securely in place, let your stitchery lines meander wherever you need them for accent or details. Antique crazy quilts are made this way, with patches firmly appliquéd on the background and wonderful stitchery wandering all over the face of the quilt. But that's the next chapter.

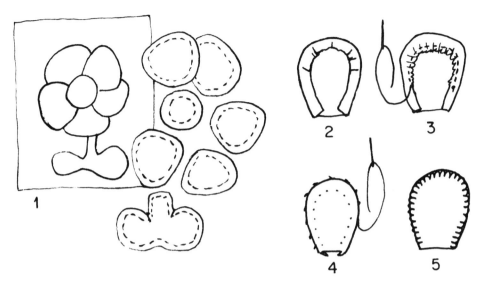

Fig. 8–11 Hemmed appliqué by hand. 1. Trace pattern pieces and add seam allowances. 2. Turn hems, except for overlapped pieces. Clip seam allowances. 3. Gather fullness with running stitches to hem. 4. Hand sew with hidden stitches. 5. Or, either hand or machine appliqué with blanket, feather, or other decorative stitch.

The Artists' Quilt

QUILT PROFILE

OCCASION: Annual exhibition of the Birmingham Society of Women Painters

GROUP: Designs by my friends in BSWP

QUILT DESIGNER: Carolyn Vosburg Hall

ORGANIZATION: Contributors were asked to make their designs in fabric to be sewn on a background square, or to create a design on paper for me to interpret in fabric.

THEME: Flowers, real or imagined

TECHNIQUE: Machine appliqué

TIME AND DATE: From fall of 1985 to fall 1986 (it was hard to get those busy painters to finish their flowers).

QUILT SIZE: 63½" × 79"

BLOCKS: 12 blocks, each 12½" square

LAYOUT: A 22″ center block with a 1½″ navy print frame, surrounded by 12 alternating 12½″-square navy and white blocks with 1½″ navy print frame; 6¼″ added batik strip on the top and a 9¼″ batik strip on the bottom; 5¼″ border all around.

COLORS: A blue-green print fabric center block, navy blue and white design blocks, navy print frames, warm brown and purple batik print strips, periwinkle outer border, and appliqué flowers in many colors.

FABRICS: Broadcloth, cotton batik, medium-weight poly-cotton.

YARDAGE: 7⅛ yards for quilt face (see Materials list for specific amounts).

QUILTING METHOD: The quilt face is machine quilted "in the ditch" directly to the blanket liner/backing, with added border quilting.

DISPLAY: Rod pocket sewn in the top border allows for hanging.

MATERIALS

(Buy extra fabric for safety margin)
Blocks:

six 13½″-square navy blocks	¾ yard
six 13½″-square white blocks	¾ yard
Center: 23″-square blue-green print	¾ yard
Frames: navy print cut widthwise and pieced	⅔ yard
four strips, 2½″ wide × 26″ long (mitered)	
four strips, 2½″ wide × 54″ long (mitered)	
Strips: batik cut widthwise and pieced	⅞ yard
one strip, 7¼″ × 54″	
one strip, 10¼″ × 54″	
Borders: periwinkle, folded lengthwise	2 yards
two vertical strips, 11″ × 69½″	
two strips, 11″ × 64½″	
Flowers: assorted plain and print fabrics	1⅓ yards
Total	7⅛ yards

Filler: 64″ × 79″ blanket trimmed to size as liner/backing *or* 64″ × 79″ poly-fiberfill with fabric backing

Other supplies: various colors of machine embroidery thread, matching sewing threads; tracing and backing paper; pins; scissors; ruler.

Fig. 8–12 Joyce Nagel added buttons to her daisy for texture on the Artists' Quilt.

PROCEDURE

1. Assemble materials and lay out all pieces on fabric lengthwise except where noted in Materials list.

2. Collect drawings or finished blocks from friends, and machine appliqué flowers on the background blocks.

3. Assemble the quilt face from the center out in this order: To the center block edges, piece and join the 1½″ frame with mitered corners (draw a 45-degree angle with a triangle on frame corners for accuracy). Join the design blocks to the frame in 2 strips of twos and 2 strips of fours. Join the next pieced 1½″ frame with mitered corners. Join the top and bottom strips to the frame. Join the 6¼″ × 69½″ side borders, then the 6¼″ × 64½″ top and bottom borders. (See Chapter 11 for details on assembly.)

4. Pin the completed quilt face to the trimmed-to-size blanket liner. Fold borders over onto back of the quilt/blanket slightly wider than quilt face border. Fold mitered corners in the border, and hand sew the mitered bottom corners. Leave the top corners open for a rod slot. Machine quilt in the ditch around each strip and block. This will also join the back border.

5. Optional: To make a quilt with filler and backing, cut the borders half as wide; piece and assemble the quilt top. Cut and seam backing pieces, and trim the bonded batting filler. Finish by joining the three layers comforter style, and machine quilt. (See Chapter 11 for assembly details, and Chapter 12 for quilting details).

Chapter 9

Embroidery by Hand and Machine
Amy's Wedding Quilt

Can you imagine that an 1890s crazy quilt, such as Louise's, might show as many as 150 different embroidery stitches? Only four basic ways to form hand embroidery stitches exist: a straight stitch, a loop stitch, a knot, and couching. Yet, combined in endless ways, nearly 300 stitches can result.

Amy's Wedding Quilt shows a variety of stitches, too. Unlike antique quilts, this one includes both hand and machine stitchery. However, that's what you might expect when twenty different people busy their needles to make quilt squares.

If appliqué patches are the cut-and-paste of fabric design, embroidery is the calligraphy. It can look like rambling colored pencil lines. like solid-color painted lines, or like decorative tracery filling in whole areas. Embroidery can be subtle in soft colors or bold in bright ones.

Embroidery combines beautifully with appliqué. The solid colors of the applied patches provide visual weight, and the mobile lines of the stitchery give accents. Judy Laslie's wedding rings on Amy's quilt combine both, and glow as richly as real jewelry in silver fabric and shiny threads (Fig. 9–2). See color section to appreciate Amy's

favorite soft pastels in the background squares. Leslie and I loved choosing them because they looked like sherbets.

We cut the fabric into rectangles for background blocks, and composed a direction sheet describing how to embroider the horizontal blocks. I added sketches of some embroidery stitches for ideas. Friends had time to make delightful blocks before the shower, and I was able to assemble the quilt enough to display at the wedding. (See my finish-before-you-finish technique in Chapter 12).

The wedding guests all loved inspecting the blocks on the quilt pinned to the wall. Hung next to the quilt was the block that came back vertical, now made into a pillow.

Planning an Embroidered Quilt

No appliqué pieces were sent with kits for Amy's Wedding Quilt, although some people added them. The major design element on this quilt is the embroidery. In addition, people added beads, sequins, ribbons and other trims.

Fig. 9–1 Amy's Wedding Quilt has a wide variety of hand and machine embroidery stitches. It was made in pastel sherbet colors: pink, melon, lavender, mint, blue, and yellow blocks on eggshell eyelet lattice and border.

Fig. 9–2 Judy Laslie made wedding rings in skillful hand embroidery and appliqué on Amy's quilt. Sisters Kim and Julie made machine-embroidered blocks, as did neighbor Mary Noonan.

Marking a Design on Fabric

This problem never goes away. How do you mark your design on fabric so it won't wear off while sewing, but it won't show later? On hand-sewn blocks you plan to wash, you can use marking that will wash out, but friendship quilts are not normally washed.

With hand embroidery not intended for washing, use a tailor's chalk pencil. It will wear off, but you can retrace it now and then as you stitch. On a very light fabric, use a very light pencil line. Be sure you sew exactly over these lines, since they are hard to remove. For no trace of leftover lines, you can hand or machine-sew long basting stitches for the design, and pull them out after you've sewn the lines.

Machine sewing is somewhat easier, since you can trace the design on tracing paper, pin it to the background, and sew through the paper. The paper tears off easily where the needle has perforated it.

Hand Embroidery

Utility sewing joins one piece of fabric to another, and decorative sewing or *embroidery* embellishes the surface, although it may also join pieces. If the needle goes in and out in one move-ment, this is *stitching*. If it goes in and is taken out in two movements, it's called *stabbing*. Stabbing is used to make close quilting stitches, for example.

Supplies

To hand embroider you need very few supplies. You need short, sharp embroidery needles with a long eye for easy threading. Next, select the colors and textures you want in embroidery flosses — cotton, shiny rayon or silk, or wool yarn for crewelwork. Cotton floss skeins usually come in six strands, loosely twisted. Rarely do you use all six at once. Commonly, you'll separate

Fig. 9–3 Hand embroidery on Louise's Antique Crazy Quilt ranges from the exquisite oriental silk embroidered flowers to the imaginative patch outlines in combination stitches. Hand embroidering names is most intricate.

131

two or three for embroidery. Cut the strands into about 15″ lengths, since a thread cut too long will tangle.

Use an embroidery hoop to hold the fabric taut while you stitch. Don't stretch the fabric within the hoop, just pull it taut without wrinkles. Be careful not to pull stitches too tightly as you sew, especially with springy wool yarns, or the finished embroidery will pucker.

The only other essentials for embroidery include good sewing scissors for clipping threads, and good light for close work.

Stitches

Directions follow for making a few of the most common embroidery stitches, with illustrations provided in Fig. 9–4. You can combine stitches endlessly to create original effects.

Back Stitch: You will use the back stitch, or variations such as the split or stem stitch, most often. A back stitch forms a solid, narrow line of thread used for outlining, embroidering your name, or stitching in fine lines.

To form this stitch, come up through the fabric at A (in Fig. 9–4), go back 1/8″ (more or less) and insert the needle at B; come up at C, 1/8″ past A. For the second stitch, insert the needle in the same hole as A, and repeat the step.

For a split stitch, the needle comes up through the thread at A. For a stem stitch, the needle comes up beside the thread at A.

Blanket Stitch: Commonly used for appliqué, the blanket stitch is formed over the edge of the applied fabric piece. It may also be used anywhere on fabric as a decorative stitch.

To make this stitch, come up at A (in Fig. 9–4) at the edge of the appliqué; insert the needle at B, 1/8″ into the appliqué, holding a small loop of thread, and come out at C, 1/8″ ahead of A along the appliqué edge. While holding the thread loop under the needle, pull the thread through and repeat the stitch.

Feather Stitch: The feather stitch is formed in a similar way to the blanket stitch (Fig. 9–4). Come up at A, forming a shallow loop. Hold the loop with your thumb and go in at B, 1/8″ to the side of A. Come up at C between A and B, 1/8″ forward, and pull the thread to form the stitch. Repeat.

Running Chain Stitch: The running chain, a series of interlocking loops, forms a wider line than the back stitch. To make the running chain, come up at A, forming a shallow loop. Insert the needle back in at A, then come up at B, 1/8″ forward of A and inside the loop. Pull the thread, but not tightly, to form a loop and repeat the stitch, going in at B and coming up inside the next loop.

Satin Stitch: Hand satin stitching consists of a series of straight stitches side by side to form a solid row.

French Knots: French knots are handy for accent stitches. To make one, come up at A. Pull the thread away from the needle and twist the needle around the thread. Insert next to A, hold the thread taut, and pull the needle through. This forms the knot.

Consult the stitch diagrams in Fig. 9–4 for other basic stitches. Use any combination of stitches to create new ones.

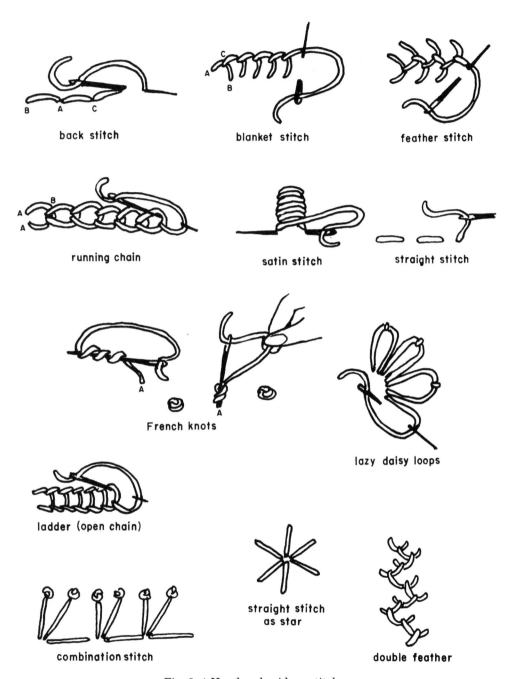

back stitch

blanket stitch

feather stitch

running chain

satin stitch

straight stitch

French knots

lazy daisy loops

ladder (open chain)

straight stitch
as star

combination stitch

double feather

Fig. 9–4 Hand embroidery stitches.

133

Machine Embroidery

The information in Chapter 8 on adjusting your sewing machine and stabilizing the background fabric applies, as well, to machine embroidery. Because any tight stitches pull on fabric, machine embroidery may require even more stabilizing than appliqué.

Preparation

In review, to stabilize fabrics, try one or more of these techniques: Add permanent lining on the back; pin removable paper on the back; stretch the fabric in a hoop; overlay the fabric with a tracing paper pattern, or plain tracing paper you can see through. One or all of these stabilizers may be used at once.

In machine embroidery, the sewing machine needle moves tiny steps forward and back, and from side to side. You do all the design guidance by assisting or overriding the feed dogs. The following stitches combine specified needle movement with various machine adjustments and your hand guidance.

Note: For free-motion stitching, where you guide the fabric in any direction you wish by hand, be very careful not to move the fabric while the needle is down. *You may pull the needle to one side, where it will hit the needle plate and break.*

Stitches

Straight Stitch: This is a simple, straightforward stitch with no unusual machine adjustments, and it is most useful. Use it for straight lines, like the supports on Dave's rollercoaster on Peter's Wedding Quilt. Use it for appliqué, to straight stitch fabric pieces in place. For a wider straight-stitch line, use a double-weight embroidery thread or two threads on top.

Free-Motion Straight Stitch: Use this wonderful technique for tracing people's signatures on the quilts. Use it also for machine basting, drawing shapes, filling in spaces, adding details to appliqué pieces, and more.

1. Set your machine for the smallest stitch length and reduce the presser foot pressure. Consult your manual for how to do this. Some machines require covering or lowering the feed dogs, and some need an embroidery or darning foot, since the presser foot pressure can't be adjusted.

2. Use an embroidery hoop to keep the fabric taut. You'll need to use permanent lining on the back of lightweight cottons.

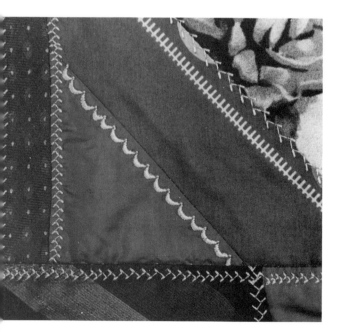

Fig. 9–5 Feather stitch, blanket stitch, and satin stitch scallops done on a Kenmore machine.

3. While doing this stitch, imagine that the needle is a pencil fixed in a holder: to draw, you must move the paper under the pencil. Use a hoop, or place your hands like an embroidery hoop on each side of the fabric in a "V" so you can control the fabric. You'll soon develop a good touch at moving the fabric exactly where you want it to go in relation to the needle.

4. Go slowly with needle speed and hand movements at first, and then gradually increase both to achieve a nice, even line.

5. To use straight stitch as a fill-in stitch, move the fabric with your hands in continuous little circles. You can overlap them for a somewhat solid area of stitching. Stitching this solidly will draw in the fabric, so keep it stabilized. Backing must be permanent, since it would be difficult to pick paper off such complex stitching.

Satin Stitch: A versatile embroidery stitch, described in Chapter 8. Use it for outlining appliqué, outlining images, and making letters. Set your machine for very short stitches, and the width zigzag you require. Loosen the top thread tension. Each thread and fabric changes the stitch, so experiment each time for the best combination. This stitch pulls in, so be sure your fabric is heavy enough to resist, and the tensions on the top and bobbin threads are loose enough.

Free-Motion Zigzag Stitch: Set your machine as for satin stitching and, in addition, release the pressure on the presser foot, or use a darning foot. This allows you to guide the fabric in any direction.

Use this stitch for two different purposes: to outline or to fill in. To out-line, reduce the presser foot pressure only halfway, so it still helps control but you can move the fabric. This means the feed dogs are still advancing the fabric, but you can guide it also. When you outline an appliqué piece this way, you won't need to turn as many corners. Just push the fabric to this side or that. Using the zigzag as a fill-in stitch effects a pencil-sketch look (Fig. 9–6).

Use this setting for sewing printed or written names. If you keep all the zigzag lines at the same angle, the signature will look like calligraphy. Study some writing done with a wide-tip, or chisel-point pen, and use the same angle. Place the writing at this slant under the needle so the angle will be on a slant.

Free-Motion Darning Stitch: If your machine will not do free-motion sewing (the old straight-stitch machines cannot) use a darning foot or spring. Both of these hold the fabric on the needle plate while the stitch forms, and then lift along with the take-up lever while the stitch is pulled tight. You can move the fabric freely during the take-up phase.

Both of these accessory feet allow for good visibility while sewing, necessary for intricate designs. Use an embroidery hoop, and permanent backing to stabilize.

Programmed Stitches: Normally, fiber artists don't have much interest in programmed stitches, since they are too regular and confining. Nevertheless, some of the stitches can be varied by width and stitch length, giving you the same look and freedom as hand embroidery.

These are the programmed stitches I

Fig. 9–6 Free-motion zigzag stitching creates the effect of a sketched pencil line on this cat by the author.

like: *the blind hem stitch*, used with a heavy embroidery thread, forms a stitch similar to a blanket stitch, and can be used to anchor hemmed appliqué.

The *feather stitch* can be varied in width and length, even while stitching. You can also guide it in large circles, spirals or whatever for a hand-sketched effect (Fig. 9–7). It looks handsewn when adjusted correctly. Using a heavy embroidery thread, I made a crazy quilt with embroidery rambling all over in one week (instead of one year) with this stitch and a few others.

I use the *scallop stitch* for quilting, for trim lines, and for details like waves in the water on Amy's Wedding Quilt, in the block showing her swimming.

Couched Stitches: When a decorative thread, yarn, or cord is too big to fit through the needle, you can lay it on the surface, then sew it down with straight, zigzag, or blind hem stitching. This is called couching. Those exquisite English and Oriental embroideries with rich gold threads are hand couched, since the gold thread is too fragile for continuous trips through the fabric. You can free-motion couch the yarn in place for fewer turns.

Stitching Signatures

Embroidering a signature is the biggest problem for most people who are asked to make a quilt block. Writing is usually small and distinctive, and hard to sew. When I'm the quilt mother, I usually offer to do it for people, and here's how to do it.

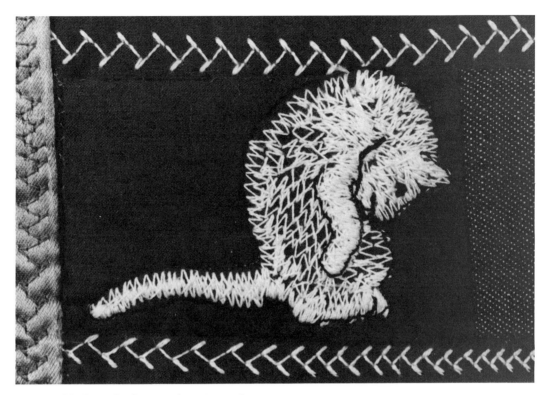

Fig. 9–7 Machine feather stitching is another way to create a sketch in fabric and stitches.

1. Ask each friend to write his or her signature on paper in ½″ high letters (capital letters to ½″ depth); pin it in place on the block.

2. Trace over the signature on translucent layout paper, using a lightbox or window if needed for accuracy. Pin the tracing on the background block. Add backing paper if needed. Use a hoop.

3. Use a clear plastic presser foot, or a darning or embroidery foot, whichever provides the best visibility. Pull the

Fig. 9–8 For machine-embroidered signatures, place paper on fabric and sew through written lines with tiny free-motion stitches, as on Mary Beard Detroit's clematis for the Artists' Quilt.

Remove paper along needle perforations.

137

bobbin thread up and pull both threads to the back, out of the way. Set your machine for free-motion straight stitching.

4. At the beginning of a line, sew a few stitches back and forth to anchor the thread. Carefully stitch the signature, following the lines on the tracing paper exactly. Where there is a break in the signature, sew back and forth to anchor threads, move to the next beginning line, anchor the threads, and continue. Keep your line as continuous as possible. For example, to sew a "t," stitch up the "t" to the cross-bar, sew out and back on the left cross-bar, sew to the top of the "t" and back to the cross-bar, sew out and back on the right cross-bar, then continue to the base line. For an "a," sew around in a circle rather than reversing. To dot an "i," go back later and stitch in place for 6 to 10 stitches.

5. When the entire signature is finished, remove the fabric from the sewing machine and trim the threads. Clip off at the fabric, or clip a longer thread and pull it through to the back by pulling on the bobbin thread. Use touches of glue to hold slippery threads like silk or rayon in place.

Satin stitch can also be used for embroidering signatures, but the lines are wider and therefore require larger-sized letters in the signature or saying. Suit the width of the satin stitch to the size of the letters in the signature.

Set your machine for free-motion zigzag, as described under "Stitches." Pin the signature tracing to the background fabric at an angle, so the satin stitch forms an attractive angle. Keep the signature at the same angle all through stitching.

Follow the lines of the signature. Just as with a wide-nib pen, some lines will be wide and some narrow. If you've picked the right angle, this will look handsome.

Finishing the Blocks

Attaching Beads, Bows and Trim

Tiny seed beads require a wire craft needle, narrow enough to fit through the tiny bead hole. Sew the beads on one at a time, or in clusters of three or four. Or you can lay a string of beads in place and "couch" them, by sewing up through the fabric every two or three beads, and catching the bead string with thread.

Sequins can be sewn on in rows as they come on a string, or one by one. You may be able to sew them on by machine.

Laces and ribbons should be appliquéd onto the fabric square with a machine straight-stitch along the edge. Since friendship quilts aren't meant to be washed, you needn't worry too much about shrinkage, but any material that is too fragile or flimsy won't hold up, so use good quality trims.

Other Kinds of Embroidery

Many other kinds of embroidery, such as needlepoint, cross-stitch, crewel, white work, drawn thread work, and raised work are popular. Inventive machine stitchers have figured out how to do most or all of these by machine. Some of these techniques appeared on individual blocks, but one was featured on an entire quilt. See Chapter 10, for Mary's Birthday Quilt.

Fig. 9–9 Jean Schuler hand-embroidered the honorees' initials (lower left), Helen Balmer machine satin-stitched the proverb (lower right), Linda Fernelius combined her free-motion signature with trims, and I machine-appliquéd and embroidered hearts.

Let's make a friendship quilt for _____

_____

to celebrate _____

on _____

   Enclosed is a fabric square for you to decorate.
Our theme for the quilt is _____.
Leave a half-inch border all around your design for me
to seam the quilt. Use embroidery floss to hand em-
broider, and a hoop to keep it smooth. Some embroi-
dery stitches are shown below.

   Use fabric or paper backing to keep the square
firm while you machine embroider it. Add ribbons,
lace, beads or other washable trim, if you wish.

   Don't forget to stitch your name on the square,
too.

   Return your quilt square to _____

_____

at _____

on _____

Embroidery Stitches

Running Stitch

Outline stitch

Feather stitch

Blanket stitch

Lazy Daisy stitch

Satin stitch

Fig. 9–10 On Amy's invitation, we provided a few hand stitches
to get everyone started.

Amy's Wedding Quilt

QUILT PROFILE

OCCASION: Wedding shower for Amy Squires and Donald Fraser

GROUP: Relatives, friends, and neighbors

QUILT DESIGNERS: Carolyn Hall and Leslie Masters Villani

ORGANIZATION: Kits included 9″ × 12″ background blocks, 9″ × 12″ iron-on interfacing for machine embroidery, and drawings of hand embroidery stitches mailed to shower guests (see Fig. 9–10).

THEME: Sayings or advice for the bride and bridegroom

TECHNIQUE: Machine or hand embroidery

TIME AND DATE: April to June, 1986

QUILT SIZE: 44″ × 80″

BLOCKS: 21 horizontal blocks, 8″ by 11″

LAYOUT: Three blocks across, seven blocks high; 2″ spacers; 3½″ side borders, 5½″ top and bottom borders

COLORS: Cream, off-white, lavender, melon, pink, light yellow, peach, light green, light blue

FABRICS: Soft poly cotton, eyelet

YARDAGE TOTALS: 11 yards (see Materials list for specific amounts)

QUILTING METHOD: Machine quilted "in the ditch" and with programmed scallop stitch

DISPLAY: Hung on the wall in the couple's new apartment

MATERIALS

(Buy extra fabric for safety margin)

Blocks: ⅓ yard each of seven background colors; cut
three 9″ × 12″ blocks widthwise from each color
fabric   2⅓ yards

Borders, sashing, backing: cream-colored eyelet   4⅓ yards
Borders: two side strips, 4½″ × 71″; two strips,
6½″ × 44″ for top and bottom
Sashing: eighteen 3″ × 12″ pieces; two 3″ × 71″
pieces
Backing: 45″ × 81″

Lining: cut all pieces to same dimensions as eyelet to
make lining for borders, sashing, and backing   4⅓ yards
                                                           _____
                              Total   11   yards

Filler: 44″ × 79″ bonded poly-fiberfill

Other supplies: machine and hand embroidery threads; cream sewing
thread; trims and laces; iron-on backing; backing paper, pins,
scissors, ruler, machine or hand embroidery hoop, embroidery
needles.

PROCEDURE

1. Lay out all pieces on fabric *length-wise* unless otherwise specified in Materials listing; cut out all pieces (½″ seam allowances are included).

2. Complete or repair blocks; change incorrectly made vertical blocks to horizontal by piecing, if possible.

3. Assemble the quilt face in vertical rows of blocks (see Chapter 11).

4. Assemble and pin the layers in this order: bonded batting, completed quilt face right-side-up, backing wrong-side-up. Sew edges and turn. (See Chapter 12 for details.)

Chapter 10

Cross-Stitch, Crayon Transfer, Stenciling, Novelty Techniques
A Quilt Quintet

The first nine chapters were devoted to traditional friendship quilting techniques, but new ideas are springing up everywhere, every day. If you want an idea for a really unusual quilt, read this chapter. It's especially appropriate if the honoree has a special skill, such as Mary's cross-stitch; or if you have friends who draw or paint, but don't sew; or if you need a quilt in a hurry.

Cross-Stitched Blocks: Mary's Birthday Quilt

My cousin, Mary Zdrodowski, yearned for a wedding quilt like Claudia's, but she already had a husband and children. When her fortieth birthday approached, we decided that was perfect for a quilt event. Mary has a zany sense of humor, so we decided on sayings and monograms for a theme. She creates original cross-stitch designs, so what better technique to choose for her quilt?

Counted cross-stitch, with its special background fabric, turned out to be ideal for letters and other linear designs, because of the orderly way it's stitched. This fabric, called Salem, Aida, or Hardanger cloth, has an open weave that corresponds to graph paper. Friends created their own designs with colored pencils on graph paper, or looked for designs already graphed. With floss-threaded tapestry needles in hand, they counted the number of holes between the open-weave threads, and stitched an "X" for each square in that color.

Many of the people invited to make squares belong to Mary's Embroiderer's Guild and were expert. Others of us were not. Mary's dad George had, to everyone's astonishment, stitched every letter in Mary's needlepoint *Enchanted Alphabet Book,* published by Annie Designs. Sister Sue had never tried cross-stitch. Our amateur blocks turned out just fine (if you don't look at the backs).

Mary's tips for cross-stitchers include keeping your work-in-process clean four ways: (1) by slipping tissue or thin fabric between the embroidery hoop and the Salem cloth; (2) by moving the hoop from place to place often; (3) by covering your work when you leave it; and (4) by working with clean hands. Also relate the size (number of strands) of embroidery floss to the fabric count (the number of holes per inch).

143

Fig. 10–1 Mary's Birthday Quilt was done in pink, white, soft green, and many colors of embroidery floss. You can see how ideal cross-stitch is for lettering.

Fig. 10–2 Even talented amateurs like Mary's sister Sue can do attractive cross-stitch. Betty's square is done from a graphed pattern in Mary's needlepoint book.

Some people can actually set their sewing machines to cross-stitch, but you'll probably use your machine only to assemble the quilt. Mary's quilt is 42½″ × 58½″, with twelve 8″ squares; it has ½″ frames around the squares, 2¾″ lattices, and 4½″ side borders, with 6½″ top and bottom borders, and a ½″ edge binding. See Fig. 3–6 for the layout diagram of Mary's quilt.

Crayon Transfer: Janet's Baby Quilt and the Kids' Quilt

What if nobody in your group can sew? Crayon transfer turned out to be an ideal solution on the Kids' Quilt and Janet's Baby Quilt. The kids in the first group were too young to be good stitchers yet, and the second group included busy advertising people who didn't have time to sew.

Claudia Stroud used this technique on a baby quilt for secretary Janet. She bought a box of Crayola brand "Fabric Colors," crayons made especially for this purpose and available at art supply stores. She says, "It was just good luck that I got the perfect fabric for the quilt, a glazed chintz." Crayon transfer colors shine brightest on synthetic or resin-coated fabrics, such as chintz. The wax of the crayons bonds with the petroleum-based resin or polyester in the fabric.

Claudia passed out white paper squares and crayons to other art directors, writers, and friends, cautioning each to remember to write backwards, *since the design reverses.* It took less than a day to collect all drawings, and another to iron them on the fabric squares and assemble the quilt.

"Janet cried when she saw the quilt at the office baby shower," Claudia

said. It now hangs over baby Candice's crib, a cheerful reminder in yellow, white, and rainbow colors of her mother's friends at her birth. The quilt is 40″ by 50″, with twelve 8″ blocks (white background squares), and 2″ lattice and 6″ borders in yellow (see color section).

Children enrolled in summer art camp at the Birmingham Bloomfield Art Association made the drawings that appear on the Kids' Quilt. Each drew a self-portrait or favorite image to iron on a tee-shirt, and Leslie Masters Villani screen-printed a frame on the shirts, then ironed each child's design inside the frame.

Since each crayon drawing can make only one print, my teen-age neighbor, Magali deVulpilliers, and her brother Michael carefully traced them onto layout paper, including "mistakes," and I ironed them onto quilt squares. I used the same top grade of glazed chintz as Claudia, especially after ironing drawings on a cotton fabric, which didn't show up well.

Transfer crayons have succinct and complete directions on the box, telling how to proceed, and it's wonderfully easy. Do pay attention to each detail so you won't iron a design on your ironing board cover, or iron crayon flecks back onto your design.

Some of the kids' camp tee-shirts went through several washings, but extreme care is recommended for cray-

Fig. 10–3 Not all stitches are crossed in cross-stitching, as Carol Fischer's saying demonstrates on Mary's quilt. Mary's father, George Vosburg, did the Z beautifully.

Fig. 10–4 Drawings for Janet's Baby Quilt were done in crayon transfer by her advertising co-workers.

on transfer. After a few vigorous washings, the resin coating will come off the chintz and the colors with it. It's best to use the quilt for display, and keep it clean so it won't need washing.

The Kids' Quilt is 49" × 65", has twenty blocks, 8" wide × 9" high, four across and five high, with 2" lattice, 5½" side borders, and 6" top and bottom borders. It takes about 4¾ yards of various colors of chintz or synthetic fabric to make the quilt. See color section for layout and details of colors.

Stenciling Hearts: Julie's Wedding Quilt

Like the one-day quilting bees of the past, Leslie planned a quilting bee at a wedding shower for Julie Squires and Greg Parry, but with a twist.

In addition to streamers, flowers, and balloons around her house, Leslie arranged a big paper-covered table surrounded by chairs in her studio. She planned to ask a few party guests at a time to come in, decorate a heart with stenciled designs, and make way for the next without interrupting the shower.

Leslie made everyone organdy aprons with their names stenciled on, and cut out heart shapes in pastel colors for people to decorate. She had already cut some stencils, and provided stencil paper and letter cutouts for others. Party goers could choose fabric markers or make stencils, stipple or brush the color on, then return to the shower.

147

Fig. 10–5 Crayon transfer makes easy, quick quilt blocks. The Kids' Quilt was made of shiny glazed chintz in bright cheery colors—hot pink, orange, purple, blue and more.

Fig. 10–6 Alexandra Winocur shows her self-portrait in crayon. Young artists in the Birmingham Bloomfield Art Association classes sketched good likenesses on white paper, ready to transfer.

That was the plan. In reality, everyone crowded into the studio, taking turns to stencil or draw with textile markers, and then stayed to kibbitz as others did theirs. No one wanted to miss the fun of this creative process.

Since this was Rosemary's second daughter to marry and we'd all been involved in several quilts by now, Leslie knew that most quilt owners hung theirs for display. She made this one an outright wall hanging: it has several layers of sheer pastel colors built up like a water color painting with no fill-er. The cutout shapes are layered between a sheer white background fabric and colored net overlay. Leslie hand embroidered around the shapes to hold them in place. The finished "quilt" hangs in a window and changes as the light comes through it, like stained glass.

The quilt measures 44″ by 57″ and has a diagram you can enlarge for patterns (Fig. 10–11). Don't worry about being exact. You can add more hearts or other shapes and move them around until they look right.

Novelty Figures: Carolyn's "SS Friendship" Quilt

Claudia and I brainstormed for ideas one day. We'd tried different ideas on various quilts for brides and friends. What else would make a successful quilt, we wondered?

"I've got it, Mom, let's make a friend's ship quilt!" We giggled at the pun and started making sketches of little felt friends crowded on a ship. The kit we mailed out consisted of the invitation to make a self-portrait (Fig. 10–14) and a 9″ × 12″ flesh-colored felt square. Not all came back by the sailing date, but with a casual design, there'll be room somewhere on the quilt for them when they do appear.

Phyllis Harrison's little figure in red and blue sailing clothes, neatly set yarn hair, and sunglasses came back first. Lori Bolt's came next, a nutty character with Brillo hair and a pink plastic suitcase. Co Abatt, a newspaper editor friend, sent herself in denim with an embroidered blouse.

My mother did herself with a pot of flowers, and Claudia included Hattie in

149

Fig. 10–7 The kids' designs were first used on their tee shirts, then retraced in transfer crayons for the quilt. Alexandra's finished portrait (from Fig. 10–6) appears at upper right, along with those of Judy, Alex, and Sandy.

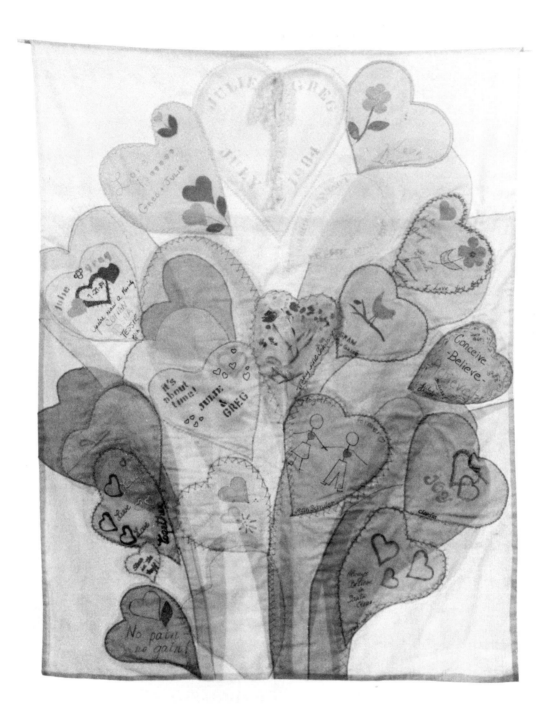

Fig. 10–8 Designs for Julie's Wedding Quilt were stenciled on sheer fabric in rainbow pastel colors. It is displayed so that window light from behind makes the colors glow.

151

Fig. 10–9 Use blunt brush to tap color onto the fabric through cutout in stencil.

her arms (see Fig. 10–13). Artist Sally Robinson dressed herself in white lace. Some friends sent drawings or suggestions, "Make me in tennis clothes."

If you make a quilt like mine, first assemble the background scene without the border, then machine appliqué or hand sew the people in place (Fig. 10–15). Next comes the border and a quilted backing (to avoid the hassle of three layers). The finished quilt measures 51″ × 67″. The side borders are 6″ wide and 6½″ top and bottom. The sky is 28″ × 39″, the water is 5″ × 39″, the dock is 2½″ × 39″, and the grass is 15″ by 39″. Use the diagram for the ship. Place your "people" wherever they look best.

13 Ideas for Terrific Quilts

- Friends could make self-portraits like the faces on the Kids' Quilt.
- People could make their own houses in a collection of fabrics, similar to

blocks on Peter's Wedding Quilt and the Birmingham Bicentennial Quilt.
- Friends could use the pattern for the pieced-block house on Hattie's Birthday Quilt, but choose their own appropriate fabric colors.
- Have people make their pets in appliqué or cross-stitch, and sign their names and the pets' names.
- Suggest that people make their favorite childhood toy.
- How about contributors making their favorite tree?
- Make a Christmas tree background and have people make signed ornaments for your tree. Add more every year.
- Collect individual signatures on strips of fabric and make a strip quilt. To do this, simply sew strips end-to-end to make strips of a given width. Then sew all the width strips together side-by-side until you achieve the size quilt you want.
- Have people sign geometric shapes such as circles, triangles, or dia-

152

Fig. 10–10 Stenciled letters give Julie and Greg advice. Embroidery stitches anchor the layers of sheer white backing and colored net overlay.

Fig. 10–11 Julie's Quilt diagram: solid lines are design units;
dotted lines are background shapes.

Fig. 10–12 I invited friends to come aboard the good ship SS Friendship. Flesh-colored felt self-portraits are machine appliquéd.

Fig. 10–13 Three additional generations join the crew: my mother, daughter, and granddaughter.

monds, and sew them on quilt squares. This can look quite contemporary in clear, bright colors.

- Collect brilliant-colored fabrics, then have your friends choose their favorite color to sign. Assemble like a crazy quilt in random shapes. Or, assemble like a rainbow.
- Consult a photography shop for directions on making photo-sensitive fabric. Then print portraits on fabric for a quilt.
- Try various unusual fabrics—leather, plastic, metallics—for an unusual quilt.
- Collect mementos from friends. Make a quilt with sheer pockets, and tuck the mementos inside where they will be visible.

Now that your head is buzzing with ideas, you'll probably come up with a fresh, original quilt. I wish I could see it. Good luck.

Please come aboard my "Good Ship Friendship"

As my special friend I'd like to have you as a passenger on my "Friend Ship Quilt" Please make yourself in felt (enclosed) about this size → in whatever pose you like.

Pin or sew fabric clothes on and sign or sew your name on. I'll applique you on the quilt.

S.S. FRIENDSHIP

Sailing date

_____

Don't be late!

With this quilt I can treasure you as my friend ALWAYS !

Thanks

Fig. 10–14 Invitation for Carolyn's "SS Friendship Quilt."

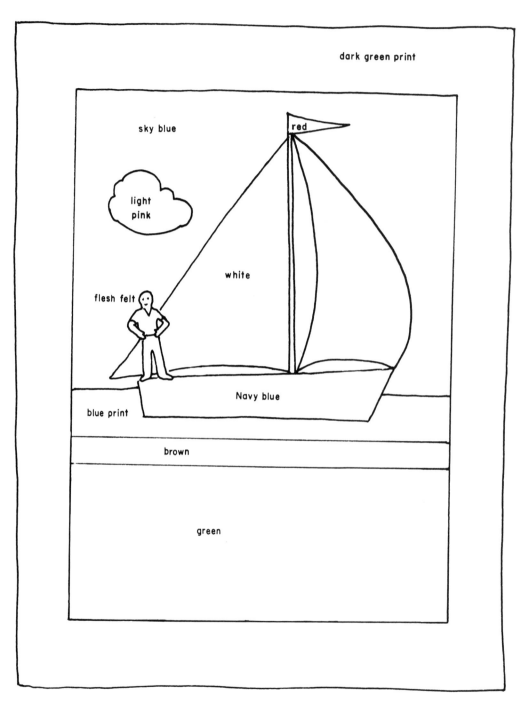

Fig. 10–15 Placement diagram and color key.

158

Chapter 11

Assembling the Quilt Face
Gini's Wedding Quilt

Here they come. By one means or another, the completed blocks return. I love seeing the blocks revealed—it's almost like opening Christmas presents. This ceremony adds excitement to wedding showers as the guests arrive with their completed blocks, and the bride discovers she will own a wedding quilt. Some friends give her their block immediately, as pleased as a child at show-and-tell. Others keep her in suspense—only when she unwraps their gift will she find the quilt block.

Lindsey Balmer presented her block with flair. She put her gift in a beautiful wicker basket, the kind Red Riding Hood always carried, and spread her block over the top. A picnic? Goodies for grandmother?

Sometimes you, as the quilt designer, will be the only one who sees the blocks until the quilt is done and presented. That's what happened with Gini's Wedding Quilt. Lois Goodrich passed out quilt block kits at the beginning of the fall semester, soon after teachers Gini and Paul announced their coming marriage. Most of the staff at Great Valley High School had taught there 15 years or more, so they all knew each other well. When their blocks were done, near Thanksgiving, everyone came to a wedding shower, including his five and her three children, for the presentation of the quilt. Can't you just hear them explaining their squares?

"The shield with the tree on top and the two blue elves on each side is your coat of arms," Lois says about her block.

Joe and Sally Kellerman's block shows the newly joined pair surrounded by all their kids. Sally Reisburg cleverly used fluffy white terry cloth for snow on her ski patrol block. If the embroidered square looks as if it took forever, it did. Art teacher Barbara Wattenmaker sewed on it all fall, while she monitored the study hall crowd. "You can't do anything else there," she said, and this battle-wise group of teachers knew just what she meant.

The new couple's eight kids, aged 15 to 19, loved the quilt the most. Lois felt all the effort that goes into making the quilt was worthwhile at that moment. But, occasionally, when confronted with some of the problems that surface, quilt designers wonder.

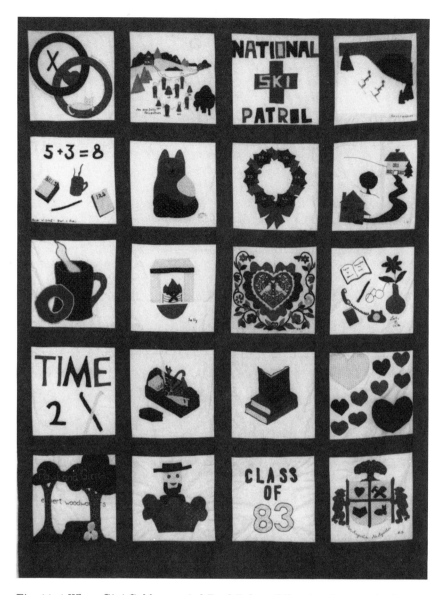

Fig. 11-1 When Gini Gable married Paul Baker, fellow teachers made them a wedding quilt in country colors — muted blue and green, soft rusty red, white, and dark brown.

Fig. 11–2 Friends on Gini's Wedding Quilt chose school-related themes to express friendship, a coffee break, and a math equation for joining their families.

Finishing and Arranging the Blocks

What if There aren't Enough?

The deadline arrives. The blocks come back, in the mail and in person, but maybe not all of them. Usually, an event like a wedding shower works well to collect blocks on time, since there's nothing like meeting a pleasurable (and public) deadline for spurring people to action. If you are missing

Fig. 11–3 Barbara Wattenmaker did this block in Pennsylvania Dutch style embroidery. It kept her busy through a term of study hall supervision.

some blocks, give those friends a call. It could be worse—you could be trying to collect blocks for a quilt without having an event to attend.

Most people don't mind the first call, in which you might ask those who have not responded whether they would like assistance. They may be embarrassed, but letting them know you value their participation may encourage them to finish their blocks, or accept your help. A second or third call may be necessary; after that, let it go. Consider others who didn't get a square, but who might like to be included.

When you've exhausted all possibilities, and you are still one square short, make an event block yourself. I've made several of these, and they turn out well because they have a specific purpose. Appliqué or embroider a large heart shape, a scroll, a circle, or other suitable design motif, and add the name(s) of the honoree(s), the date, the event, and other relevant information. This may turn out to be the cornerstone block.

Make blocks for missing friends or relatives. On Peter's Wedding Quilt, I made a square for my Dad. We all remembered him fishing off the dock, sometimes with a clacking pelican waiting for a handout. Yes, sentimental squares have a rightful place on friendship quilts. On the earliest friendship quilt (The Trenton Quilt, 1839), the squares cover a span of more than 20 years, and many of its sayings offer virtuous advice or touching sentiments.

Before you design additional blocks, lay out the ones you have and see how they look together. Your added block can enhance the overall quilt design. For example, if one block is much different in visual weight, style, or technique than the others, your added block may be able to balance it.

What if You Have Too Many?

First, reshuffle. I'll agree that a 21-block quilt (3 by 7 blocks) is a stranger shape than a 20-block quilt (4 by 5 blocks). For a long, narrow quilt, perhaps you can add side borders or use it as a wall hanging like Amy's Quilt. See Chapter 3 for layout ideas.

When no possible way to reshuffle the blocks remains, consider making the orphan extra block into a pillow. This happened on quilts where friends disregarded the instructions, using an entirely different technique. We still loved their squares, so we made pillows of them.

Inspection and Repairs

Assuming you have just the right number of blocks, inspect them to see if they need any repairs, embellishment, or reworking. It's unlikely that all twenty or more contributors are expert seamstresses, and a little help might be in order.

If you feel the block-maker might resent your additions, ask him or her to fix it. When Claudia made the crayon transfer baby quilt, one man's square pictured a beer mug. She asked him to redo it; he did, and the quilt is delightful. If some blocks are unusual or not so skillful, don't worry. Once the blocks are combined, individual peculiarities of design or stitching tend to blend into an effective whole.

Puckered blocks will give you problems. Don't sew them into a quilt along existing seam lines. Puckering, like quilting, draws the edges in and makes the block smaller and distorts it. Remove the puckered stitches on machine appliqué, for example, and replace them, if possible. If not, press the block as flat as you can without stretching it. On the back, redraw the seam lines with a template. Wrinkles may show, but this is preferable to distorting the overall quilt. Another solution is to stitch the puckered block to a flat backing square, and add trapunto stuffing to fill in the gathers.

Sometimes people may glue on materials that you know won't last out the week. Ask if you can replace them with something else. You can also appliqué the sheerest fabric you can find over the glued items to keep them safely in place.

Before assembling the quilt, check to see if beads or other solid objects extend over seam lines. You won't be able to sew over them by machine, so remove them before you stitch.

Seam Allowances

Turn the completed blocks over and draw seam lines in pencil around the perimeter (Fig. 11–4). Use a cardboard template the exact size and shape of the completed block. Hold the template in place with one hand, and pull the angled pencil toward you to avoid "skipping." If the block back has other lines on it, make yours in an identifiable color of wax pencil. Don't draw any of the lines too hard, since they may show through or smear.

Two common mistakes happen on blocks. On a fabric square given out with a nice, wide 1″ seam allowance, people often forget the seam allowance and design right to the edge. On these, you'll need to draw the seam allowance on the back no matter, and risk covering some of the design. You may be able to shift the block template around to include the most important parts of the design, or redo parts to get them inside the frame.

The second common mistake occurs when you ask for a certain size block and it comes back with no seam allowances. Sometimes this happens even with blocks you send out. It's ingenuity time. Can you seam strips of fabric to the edges for a border? Can you appliqué decorative ribbon to the edges

Fig. 11–4 Mark seam allowance around a cut-to-size template on the back of finished quilt blocks, pulling the pencil at a low angle to avoid rucking fabric.

like a frame? Can you appliqué the block onto another background square?

Double-Check Border Fabric

One last thing before assembling the quilt face. I hope you haven't cut out all the sashing and border pieces. Before doing so, spread out the blocks next to the border and lattice fabric and see how it looks. Do the blocks still look good with the border fabric you bought a couple of months ago? Friends may have added enough unusual embellishments to alter the color scheme, and you will need a different border and lattice.

Does the honoree like the border fabric? Kim's Valentine Quilt got new border fabric, and we all liked it better. Lois shopped for the perfect blue for Gini's quilt in store after store, carrying along her packet of finished blocks while completion day neared.

The reason you don't simply wait to choose border fabric is that friends like to know the color range, and including a swatch of border fabric in the appliqué packets incorporates the colors.

Balance and Symmetry

Lay out the blocks where you are able to see them all at once. Put them on the floor, on a bed or table, or tape them up on the wall. Then get a cup of tea and sit down to contemplate the blocks. (I spread them on the floor and stand on the counter in my studio, but my husband doesn't think it's safe for me to recommend this.) If the floor or wall is quite different in color from the border fabric, lay or tape the border fabric up first and put the blocks on it.

What are you looking for? First think about the imagery and the technique used on the blocks. Those that are too different may be jarring next to each other. A saying may look odd next to a realistic image, a carefully hand-sewn block may destroy the effect of a more primitive block. It's not fair to put all the "good" blocks on one side. They should be spread out. Spreading similar blocks around the quilt will probably be more effective than grouping them.

Now squint your eyes to see if the blocks balance. You'll notice the colors first. Are they sprinkled around the quilt evenly, or are all the reds in one corner? Shift the blocks back and forth to ascertain the best effect.

Squint again and look at the shapes of the motifs. Different design elements make different visual demands. Circles draw you into them like a bull's-eye in a target (so do bright reds). An X design has a similar effect (Fig. 11–5). Blocks with large amounts of dark colors are "heavy." Blocks that are markedly different from all the others may be hard to place.

Design shapes often create movement. Symmetric shapes like circles, Xs and squares stay put, but curved lines, triangles, or clusters of dots will all cause your eye to move in some direction (Fig. 11–6). Find these movements within each block and use them in the overall arrangement.

I don't mean for this to sound incredibly complicated. You may come up with a wonderful final arrangement instinctively; on the other hand, some quilts require a lot of shuffling to achieve balance. I commonly put "heavy" blocks in the middle or on lower corners, and symmetric blocks up the center row. If blocks have angular movement, like the diagonal "Amish Square" at the lower right of Hattie's Birthday Quilt. I make sure

the direction of movement stays within the quilt. Crazy quilts commonly have a version of "Grandmother's Fan" in the corners (see Louise's Antique Crazy Quilt).

When you are balancing the squares, pretend they have actual weight and the whole thing will tip over if you don't balance it properly. To keep the design from getting bottom heavy, remember those wonderful balancing acts at the circus. The more incredible they are, the more exciting!

Don't rush. Along with picking the colors, this is one of the most important steps. When you do it well, nobody notices, but the quilt looks harmonious. If the balance is off, it nags at the viewer.

Now for the big step: assembling the quilt face.

The Strip Assembly Technique

Here's a step-by-step procedure for assembling the quilt. The first two steps repeat some of the previous discussion.

Step One: Preparation

1. Make sure each block is large enough. If not, frame it with extra matching or coordinating fabric sewn on.

2. Press the block flat. Repair puckers or the other problems.

3. Lay out the blocks in a pleasing arrangement.

4. On the back of each block, trace around a cardboard template the exact size of the finished block, drawing a seam line lightly with pencil.

5. On the back of each lattice

Fig. 11–5 Study visual movement of block designs. Blocks with central X or O shapes draw attention just like a bull's-eye, as does this photo-transfer block from Lori's Wedding Quilt.

(sashing, divider, intersection) trace around a cardboard template the exact size of the finished lattice, drawing a seam line on the back of the lattice lightly with pencil. You *cannot* assume that you can eyeball the seam allowance on the lattice and borders because they are straight edges. This is *not accurate* (sez I, who did it that way and had to take it out).

6. If intersections—corners where lattice pieces meet—are used, make a

template the size of the finished intersection and trace a pencil line on the back of each intersection.

7. On the back of each strip lattice, use a yardstick or metal ruler to draw two full-length seam lines the distance apart of the finished lattice. Measure with ruler or templates, and mark at each point where block and lattice seams will join. Draw right-angle lines across or measure each side, whichever is more accurate.

8. On the back of each border piece, measure and draw seam lines with a yardstick or ruler. If block and lattice seams adjoin, mark these places. If not, mark end seams and the middle to check for accuracy.

9. As you sew seams together, keep checking dimensions with a tape or ruler.

Step Two: Organize and Diagram

The directions for each quilt tell you if the blocks are assembled in vertical or horizontal strips (in some cases this is not relevant). In my directions, this is related to how the pieces fit best on the yardage. You may wish to change this layout and make the longest possible strips.

1. Lay out all parts of the quilt face as they will be sewn together. This will allow you to see if the quilt looks the way you planned. This is your last chance to make changes. Make a diagram on graph paper showing where every piece goes. It's so easy to forget the order you planned. I can get scrambled brains even with my blocks all stacked neatly, so I recommend a diagram.

2. Stack the blocks and lattice by

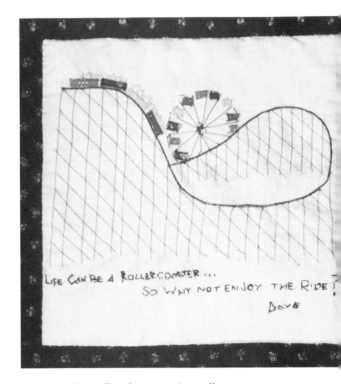

Fig. 11–6 Visually, the swooping roller-coaster line moves your eye around Dave's block on Peter's Wedding Quilt.

rows. To do this, on each row of blocks with the equal length lattice, flip the lattice over face to face on the block, then start at the bottom to stack that row of blocks with each lattice. Begin at the bottom of the next row and stack the blocks and lattice, and put the finished pile at an angle on top of the first blocks. Keep going in this manner until you have stacked the whole quilt, angling each pile of blocks to keep them separate. You can stack all blocks in one pile and all lattice in another as some books recommend, but you must remember whether or not the end blocks have lattice joined.

167

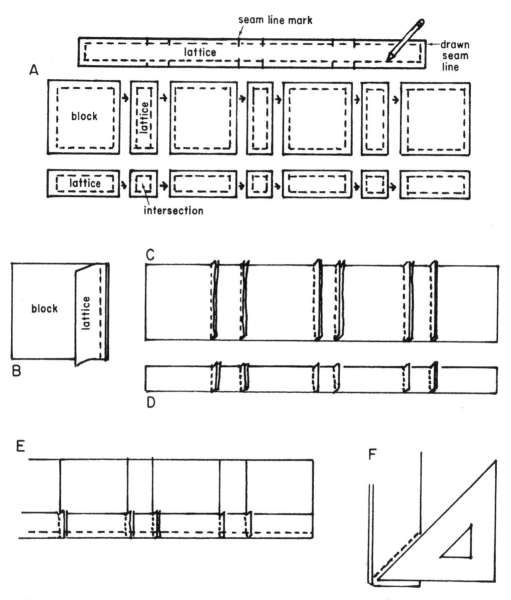

Fig. 11–7 Assembling the quilt top. A. Draw seam lines and joining marks on blocks and lattice. Lay out blocks and lattice in strips. B. Align block and lattice on drawn seam lines, pin, and stitch. C. Assemble alternating blocks and lattice in strips. D. Assemble alternating lattice and intersections in strips. E. Join assembled block/lattice rows to lattice/intersection rows by matching seams. Sew. F. For mitered corners, draw seam line at a 45° angle with triangle.

3. If you have intersections in your layout, stack them as you did the blocks and lattice. If not, fold and stack the strip lattice in a pile and the borders in another. Label top and bottom borders if needed. Now you can store the quilt until you are ready to sew without forgetting what goes where.

Step Three: *Stitching Blocks to Lattice*

1. Join the first lattice to the first block in the pile of blocks. To do this, align the lattice face to face with block and put a pin through each corner seam line (marked in pencil) on the block and lattice. One pin at each corner may not be enough to keep the entire seam line perfectly aligned, so add enough pins to do this. Stitch the seam by hand or machine (Fig. 11-7A). Turn it over and see if stitches follow the seam line exactly. If not, restitch. (Sorry about that, but you will care later if they aren't accurate.) Repeat for all but the last block in the row, unless it also has a lattice. If it does, the block will have top and bottom pieces of lattice attached. Remove pins as you come to them in sewing, or sew over them if your machine will do this, and then remove the pins.

2. Join the row of blocks and lattice together. To do this, align the first lattice with the second block, as accurately as described above, and stitch. Continue joining lattice to blocks to create a continuous row of blocks and lattice (Fig. 11-7C). Repeat this step for all horizontal rows of blocks.

3. If your quilt has intersections instead of a long strip lattice, make a strip of intersections and lattice. To do this, join the end of a lattice to an in-tersection, pinning accurately on seam lines. Continue joining alternate intersections and lattice until the row contains the same number of intersections and lattice as the block strips (Fig. 11-7D). Repeat this step for all lattice rows.

Step Four: *Joining the Rows and Lattice*

1. Press completed block/lattice rows and lattice/intersection rows. A steam iron works best to keep seams flat. Press the seams to one side for hand stitching or loose machine stitching. If fabric is heavy and machine-sewn, it may look better to press seams open.

2. Align the first block/lattice row with a strip lattice or lattice/intersection row, face to face. Match seams *carefully and accurately*, pin at right angles to the seam line, and stitch (Fig. 11-7E). Open the seam to check intersection joinings for accuracy. Redo if necessary.

On continuous-strip lattice, align the block/lattice seams with the marks drawn on the strip lattice; pin at right angles and stitch.

3. Repeat the steps above to join each block/lattice row with each lattice row.

4. Press the completed block section seams, to one side or open. Clip excess fabric from seam joinings so the quilt will lie flat. Check for secure seams and measure for accuracy. Redo any faulty seams.

Step Five: *Joining the Borders*

1. Most likely, side borders will be joined next. Check your quilt layout to make sure. Align the side border with the side of the assembled blocks and

lattice. Pin the seam lines accurately, matching marks and seams, and stitch. Repeat for the other side. Press.

2. Join the top and bottom borders in this same manner.

3. If there is more than one border, as on the Minister's Retirement Quilt, keep on joining in the same manner until the quilt face is finished. Press seams open.

Step Six: Mitering Corners

1. If the borders are joined with mitered corners, as are the corners of the narrow striped border on the Artists' Quilt, mark the angle of miter carefully with a 45-degree triangle (Fig. 11–7F). (Or make a square of paper the width of the border and fold it diagonally for a 45–degree angle.)

2. Assemble these mitered borders as if making a frame by sewing the corners together at the angles first. You must be very accurate. Stitch from the outer edge to the seam line only on the inside corners, so the seam allowances will open. Press the seams open.

3. Pin the border frame to the assembled blocks, matching block corners exactly with the mitered corner seam line. For machine sewing, stitch to the corner, block side up, and stop with the needle down in the fabric at the exact corner.

4. Turn the corner in this manner: the open seam allowances of the miter allow for shifting the fabric to align the next seam. Pivot the fabric on the needle, align the next seam flat, and sew to the next corner. Repeat.

5. If you should happen to have a double border with each corner mitered, join the border strips first, then sew the mitered corners together, and finally sew the frame on the quilt.

Step Seven: Finishing the Quilt

Seam the backing if needed, and press. The face and backing are now ready to quilt. Chapter 12 provides the details on quilting stitches and binding the edges. Don't fold that finished top away "until you have plenty of time to quilt." Read my new, fast, finish-before-you-finish technique.

Gini's Wedding Quilt

QUILT PROFILE

OCCASION: The finished quilt was presented at an after-school wedding shower for teachers Gini Gable and Paul Baker.

GROUP: Fellow teachers at Great Valley High, Malvern, Pennsylvania

QUILT DESIGNER: Lois Vosburg Goodrich

ORGANIZATION: Each kit included a background square and appliqué swatches

THEME: Shared ups and downs at Great Valley High School

TECHNIQUE: White muslin background fabric blocks with appliqué fabric swatches provided, were embellished as friends chose. This included appliqué by hand and machine, embroidery by hand and machine, and a trapunto tree scene. Added fabrics include fluffy terry cloth for snow.

TIME SPAN: Kits went out at the beginning of the fall semester. By the due date at the end of October, blocks were completed. Quilt completed November 20.

SIZE: 59¼" × 78¼"

BLOCKS AND LAYOUT: Twenty blocks, 12" square, 4 across, 5 high; 2¼" lattice, 2¼" border, and 7" bottom border

COLORS: Off-white cotton background blocks; appliqué designs in plain rust, off-white print, medium blue print, dark green print, rust pindot, dark brown print; border and lattice, medium-blue pindot, white binding

FABRIC: Quilting cottons

YARDAGE TOTAL: 12 yards of quilting cottons, plus a double-sized sheet for backing

FILLER: Bonded polyester quilt batt

QUILTING METHOD: Edges finished but yet to be quilted

DISPLAY: Wall hung

Chapter 12

Assembling and Quilting the Layers
Colleen's Wedding Quilt

"Quilting organizes the wrinkle pattern." The other, more utilitarian, purpose is to fasten the three layers of a quilt together.

Nothing slows completion of a friendship quilt more than the process of quilting (unless it's not getting the blocks back). Several quilts tracked down for this book had finished tops, but they weren't yet quilted and couldn't be shown. The fun part was done, and only toil remained.

This problem is not new. Louise's Antique Crazy Quilt was left unfinished from 1898 until I received it about 10 years ago, in spite of the fact that this type of quilt typically was "knot quilted," an easy, quick method.

Quiltmakers have coped with the time, space, and energy-consuming process of quilting in a number of ways. Hand quilters use full-width quilting frames or large hoops, or design their quilts in smaller units. It's even possible to quilt with no hoop if you baste or pin liberally.

People like me who like things done fast use the sewing machine to quilt. I use a slam-bang style of quilting, closest to "comforter style," that I call my finish-before-you-finish method. Briefly, the three quilt layers are laid

wrongside out, machine-seamed around three edges, and turned. With these finished edges, you can do the quilting when you get around to it. No unfinished quilt faces around here. This method can be combined with machine or hand-quilting to good effect, as on Lori, Peter, and Hattie's quilts. Details of this technique follow later in this same chapter.

While photographing quilts for this book, we intentionally diffused our lights to highlight the detailed design blocks and to de-emphasize the quilting puffs. "Too bad," you might think, yet only a few of the many quilts shown are fully quilted. Nearly everyone – including me – instinctively eliminates excess quilting stitches on friendship quilts because the surface detail on the design blocks gets lost in the quilting valleys, especially with the loftier polyester fiberfill batting.

Even the earliest friendship quilts were not as fully quilted as their contemporaries, since they were keepsakes and not intended for heavy use. Mary Stilber, a noted quilt collector and expert, says that quilts need some quilting, or the fabrics will sag over the years. Her Trenton Quilt, probably the earliest authenticated friendship quilt,

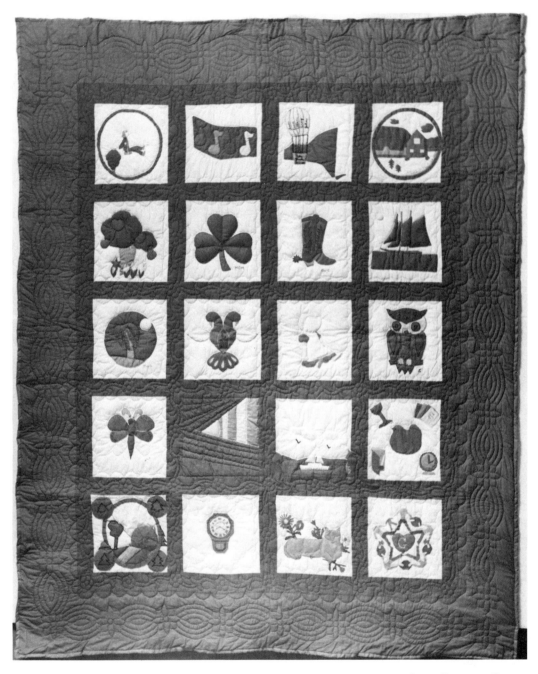

Fig. 12–1 On Colleen's Wedding Quilt, the dimensional pattern comes from all-over quilting stitches. Colors are muted in blue, green, tan, pink, and rusty red.

173

dated 1839, is quilted in an all-over floral pattern, but not too solidly (Fig. 12–2).

Several ways to quilt by hand and machine follow. I've emphasized my finish-before-you-finish method, the one I use for friendship quilts, because it has several advantages and is the quickest. Other methods are mentioned briefly. The Suggested Reading list includes several quilting books that provide extensive details on these and other quilting techniques.

There's one more option to mention, if you prefer traditional hand quilting: take it to a professional quilter or group to finish.

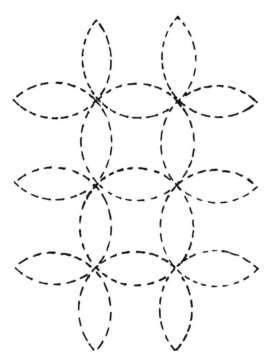

Fig. 12–2 The Trenton Quilt's "daisy" pattern. Quilting patterns should be evenly balanced so the "drawing-in" is even in all directions.

Professional Quilting

The face of Colleen's Wedding Quilt was stitched and assembled by a group of friends in Pennsylvania, and then taken into the nearly Pennsylvania Dutch Country for quilting. You can tell from the imagery that this quilt was made in that area, and that the quilting was done by experienced hands.

Lois Goodrich was the quilt designer, assembling and dispersing the kits, collecting the blocks, and assembling the top. Lois enlisted Sadie, an Amish quilter in Goodville, Pennsylvania, to do the quilting. Sadie charges by the yard of thread for her services, as do other women in Goodville (ZIP code 17528), Churchtown (ZIP code 17510) and other Dutch country communities. She quilts on a large quilting frame and may get help from family and friends. Many women in the area will be happy to quilt for you. Write to the town post offices mentioned above, or consult the ads in quilting magazines for those offering quilting services.

Designers of the Minister's Retirement Quilt took it to the Grass Roots Co-Op in Lost Creek, Kentucky 41348, for quilting; Elaine Morse says it cost about $100 at the time. On that particular quilt, with 6" squares, the stitching pattern of overlapping circles around the blocks created a cozy effect.

Over the years, exacting standards of acceptance and excellence for quilting have developed. In the days of hand quilting, with thin cotton batting and soft-weave cotton fabrics, quilting rows less than 2" apart and 12 stitches per inch were considered acceptable. Rows one inch apart and 18 stitches

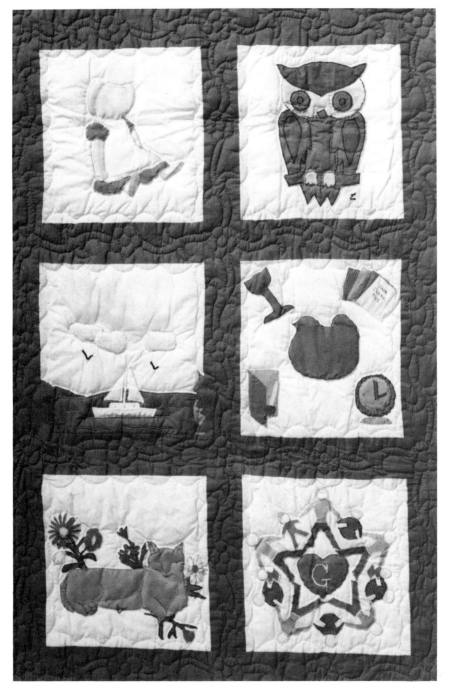

Fig. 12–3 Quilting stitches outline shapes and create three-dimensional patterns in the lattice.

175

per inch ranked as perfection. That's why a lot of quilt tops go unquilted. Thank goodness friendship quilts don't need this much quilting, since quilting pattern textures often compete with the design blocks.

Colleen's Wedding Quilt shows large, simple design motifs well-suited to quilting. The stitches are done in flower and leaf patterns around the border and on the lattice. Each quilt block is outline-quilted according to its own pattern. Distances between quilting rows average from 1 to 2 inches. About 6 or 7 stitches per inch are used because the batting is too puffy for closer stitching.

This quilt benefits from the added texture, because quilting valley shadows delineate the design motifs better than the light-colored appliqué stitching. When designing quilts, be sure to suit the quilting pattern to the design pattern. A well-designed quilt brings great pleasure to its new owners.

Colleen's completed quilt arrived at the bride's home a week before the wedding and became the star of the wedding gift display, a chance for everyone to "meet" all the friends and relatives. Lois said Peter's Wedding Quilt did the same thing—drawing family and friends together as they told what each block meant. Colleen's 25-year-old brother, owner of the cat in the flowers, pronounced it the nicest wedding gift he had ever seen.

Motifs show family interests, sail-

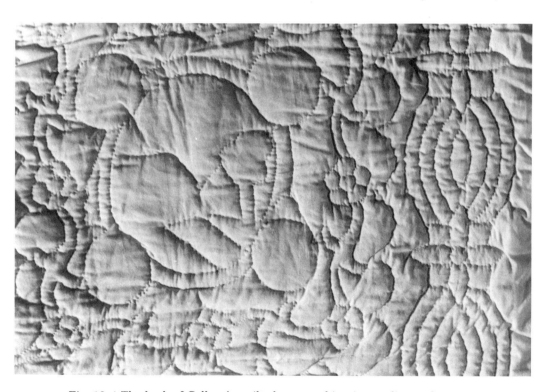

Fig. 12–4 The back of Colleen's quilt shows combination outline and pattern stitching, done by expert Amish quilters.

ing, skiing, and even clock collecting; sister-in-law Debby made the cowboy boot; some blocks show a strong Pennsylvania Dutch influence. Acting as quilt designer is a big undertaking, but one Lois was happy to do for Colleen, her first home economics student to follow in that profession.

Making a Quilt Sandwich

Fillers

Once the quilt face is done, the next step is to assemble the quilt. This three-layer sandwich includes top, filler, and backing. Some choice exists as to materials for filler. Quilters of the past used cotton batting, wool batting,

Fig. 12–5 The clover leaf puffs into appealing shapes from the lofty fiberfill batting and the outline quilt stitches.

a blanket, or even horse hair, corn husks, or a newspaper layer (sometimes used as templates and left in for warmth).

Most machine quilters use bonded polyester batting. This synthetic fiber is lightweight, washable, maintains its loft better than cotton batting, is reasonable in cost, and easy to work with. The bonded batting has fibers fused together to prevent the filler from shifting, so less quilting is needed. It's available everywhere in batts sized from single bed up, and comes in different thicknesses. For most friendship quilts, the thin single-weight batt will work best so the quilt is not too puffy or heavy and is easier to handle.

Hand quilting works best with a very thin, non-bonded batt, which requires closer quilting stitches to keep the filler from shifting. Unbonded batting, glazed batting (resin coated only on the outsides), and bonded batting come in bags, rolls by the yard, and prepackaged. Read the label on packaged batting carefully to be sure what you are buying.

Two-layer quilts avoid the use of a separate batting. On Lori's quilt, I used a prequilted printed fabric, the kind with the batting already quilted firmly to it. The Artists' Quilt has a soft blanket backing, also eliminating the need for additional batting. These two-layer quilts lay very flat and are easy to hand or machine quilt.

Backings

Use a light- to medium-weight cotton or cotton-poly blend for backing. Sheets make good backings for machine-sewn quilts because seams are usually not needed, but they may be too difficult for hand quilters to push a

177

needle through. Buy the next largest sheet size and preshrink it for your quilt backing. If this is your first machine sewn quilt, buy a nice busy small print so mistakes don't show.

The Finish-Before-You-Finish Method

This quick method combines the three layers, wrong sides out, machine sewing around the edges leaving an opening, and turning the quilt with the batting now inside (Fig. 12–6). The advantages are several. It's fast. The quilt looks finished enough for display even before it is quilted. The finished border makes a bold frame without a binding. You can quilt it at your leisure, choosing any of several quilting techniques: knot it, free-motion machine quilt, or hand quilt with or without a hoop.

The reasons traditional quilts are not made this way are several. Unwanted wrinkles or extra fabric can be accommodated while quilting from the center out. Quilting, especially on thick batting, "draws in" the quilt. Elaborate quilting patterns may draw the quilt unevenly. Raw edges allow for trimming back to straight edges after quilting.

For several reasons I don't use this raw edge method. Primarily, I don't want to alter the geometry of a design, pull the quilt out of true by pushing fabric to the edges, nor distort it by over-quilting. My quilts usually hang square and flat. Further, I don't want to wrestle with a huge quilting frame. With finished edges I can keep quilting

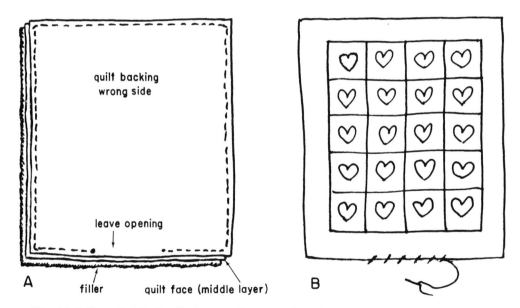

Fig. 12–6 No unfinished quilt faces with my finish-before-you-finish technique. A. Join quilt layers on the wrong side, seam the edges, trim and turn. B. Sew the opening closed, and finish quilting at your leisure.

as long as I wish. That's both sides of the quilting debate, imagery versus stitchery. Choose your own technique from the following.

Assembling Layers with Finished Edges

1. Find an area large enough to lay out the whole quilt — the floor or a ping pong table. Assemble these tools and supplies:

Steel safety pins
2″ plastic-headed quilting pins
Long shears
Carpenter's square or T-square
Masking tape

2. First lay the quilting batt on the floor or a table and smooth it flat, but do not stretch it. If the batt needs piecing, peel back half the thickness for an inch from each of the adjoining edges and trim it off to avoid a double-thick area. Overlap these edges and hand baste with long stitches that do not depress the batting.

3. Measure the quilt top to see if opposite sides match in length. Draw seam lines on the back around the edges. Lay the completed quilt top right-side-up on the batting. Square the quilt. To do this on a rug, use the long pins at an angle to pin the quilt top to the rug. Pin one top corner, pull the quilt taut, and pin the other. Use the T-square to true the corners; make sure not to pull fabric off-grain or out of shape. Smooth and pull the face taut and pin the lower corners, always checking to see that it remains square. On a hard surface, use masking tape to hold it in place, and use the floor tile lines or table edges to check for square (Fig. 12–7).

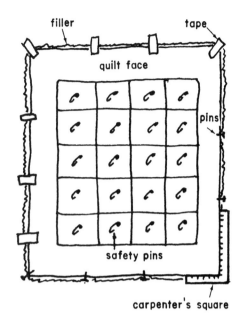

Fig. 12–7 To "square" the quilt face, pin it to carpet or tape it to the floor over the filler. Measure sides and check for square.

4. Using safety pins, pin the top to the batting at 6″ to 12″ intervals. You are probably going to have to crawl all over the quilt, so check your knees for grass stains and shoes for Cheerios. Trim the batting to within 1″ of the edge all around.

5. Draw edge seam lines on the reverse side of the backing. Lay the backing on the quilt top, right sides facing, and smooth tautly in place. Pin or tape it at the corners as before and check to see that it's square and fits the top. Using 2″ quilting pins, pin at right angles to the edge every 6″ all around the perimeter, aligning the drawn seams.

6. Unpin or untape the quilt from the floor or table, and take it to the sewing machine. Check the seam line and repin where needed without shift-

179

ing the fabric more than a fraction of an inch. The wrong side of the backing is on top, and the batting on the bottom. Ease the pressure on your sewing machine presser foot if necessary. If the batting catches on anything, back it with tissue paper or newspaper, but the bonded batting should sew just fine. Hold the seam in front of and behind the needle to keep the layers even.

Note: To make a rod slot, see instructions below before completing step 7.

7. To sew, use a medium-length stitch, about 8 stitches per inch. Begin on the bottom edge in the center and stitch toward the corner. At the corner, stop one stitch short, angle across the corner with two stitches, and begin stitching up the side (Fig. 12–8A). This makes a square corner and allows room to accommodate the fillers and seam allowance when turned. Sew each corner this way. Stitch all around the quilt, but stop 18″ from the beginning stitching (Fig. 12–8B).

8. Lift the backing fabric across the opening at the bottom of the quilt. Sew the quilt face border to the batting across this opening, stitching outside the seam line and within the seam allowance (Fig. 12–8B).

9. Trim the seam allowances: trim off all the filler close to the seam line; trim the top seam allowances to ¼″ and the backing to ½″. Make an angle cut across each corner, coming within an ⅛″ of the stitching. If your fabric is not firmly woven, reinforce the corner with added stitching.

10. Turn the quilt right-sides-out, filler in. To do this, poke each top corner into the quilt and out the bottom opening. Gently pull the quilt through. If the quilt is too bulky to turn, remove some stitches. The safety pins will hold the batting to the top. Poke the bottom corners through. Flatten out the quilt and check every seam for folds, puckers—whatever flaw— and restitch if necessary.

11. Pin the opening closed and hand stitch with hidden stitching, covering the stitches that hold the batting and face. Press the edge seam flat by finger or iron; pin at right angles to the edge. (Don't iron if your batting fuses when

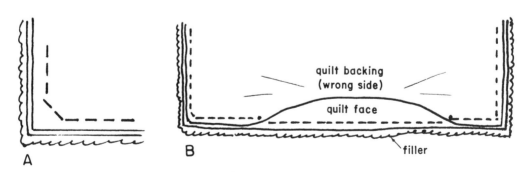

Fig. 12–8 A. To sew the stacked and pinned or basted quilt sandwich edges, follow drawn seam lines, and angle across corners. Leave an opening as shown in 12–6. B. Lift the quilt backing fabric across the opening and sew the quilt face to the filler in the seam allowance to anchor the filler.

180

heated!) Use a long hand-stitch, or machine-baste to sew around the edges 1" or so from the edge.

12. Repin or tape the quilt to the floor, making sure it is smooth, taut, and square. Fluff up the quilt to remove folds from the batting, if necessary. Once the quilt is smooth and held firmly, remove the safety pins one at a time and repin, including all three layers. Do not pin over a quilting line. Insert more safety pins to keep the layers even, as needed. Now you are ready to quilt.

Making a Rod Slot

To make a rod slot at the top of the quilt, make the seam corners in the following manner *before you stitch* in step 7, above.

1. Sew up the first side to within 2" of the top; backstitch.

2. Sew across the top, beginning off the fabric and stitching a straight seam across the top, ending off the fabric. This fabric will be turned and needs a complete seam (Fig. 12–9).

3. Begin 2" down on the opposite side, backstitch, and continue sewing the edges as in step 7, above.

4. Skip to step 9 above and continue: *Do not trim the top corners at an angle,* nor the seam allowances at the rod slot opening. Trim off the filler across the top seam. Press the seam open (fingers will do) and turn the seam allowance back at the top corners on the seam line. To complete, hem the rod slot by hand, stitching the fabric to the batting with long, angled stitches to hold it firmly (Fig. 12–9B). Do not sew quilting stitches through the rod slot.

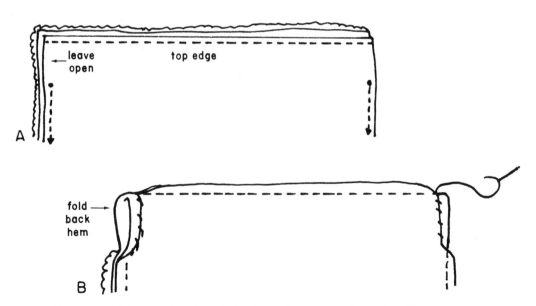

Fig. 12–9 Making a rod pocket. A. In the quilt top edge, leave the side-top corners unstitched when seaming the edges. B. Turn back the unstitched side-top seam allowances and hand hem.

181

Assembling Layers with Raw Edges

The process is essentially the same as above, except that the layers are combined right-sides-out. To do this, read the steps above for details and then assemble your layers in this fashion.

1. Lay out and smooth the quilt backing, right side down on the floor or ping pong table. Make sure it's "squared" and not pulled off-grain. Pin or tape in place.

2. Lay the batting over the backing and smooth in place without stretching. Trim the batting to backing edge.

3. Lay out and smooth the assembled quilt top on the batting, aligning the seam lines on the quilt top with the quilt backing. Pin or tape the quilt top taut and smooth.

4. Use safety pins to baste the quilt every 6" or so, including all edges. Now you are ready to quilt.

Machine Quilting

Machine quilting is faster than hand quilting, but fast is relative. If it takes a month to hand quilt, it may take several days to machine quilt. I'm always sold on my own propaganda and think I'll finish everything in 25 minutes (and then spend hours and days and days on my hot ideas). Never mind being more realistic. Such optimism gives me confidence to plunge ahead.

The faster you race down those rows of machine quilting, the greater the chance you will have tucks on the back and pulls on the front and have to take the stitching out. Use all the care and skill you can muster at each step to get it perfect the first time through. As a general guideline, use longer stitches since they are easier to take out and don't puff the quilt so much.

Get yourself and your machine ready for the big project. Don't start out on a king size quilt, or even a double. Try a crib quilt first. You can concentrate on developing skills and succeeding quickly, without wrestling bulk.

Controlling Bulk

Arrange your sewing machine on or near a table to support the weight and size of the quilt while you sew. It would be ideal to have someone feed the quilt to you, but these people are hard to come by. I still get a kick out of Robbie Fanning's story about the kids on each corner of a quilt, running to and fro as their mother ordered.

To sew in the center of the quilt, roll both ends of the quilt and tie or pin the roll in place. Be sure the quilt is well basted with pins or hand basting first, because rolling will cause the layers to shift. If layers appear to shift anyway, accordian-fold the ends and tie a cord around these bundles (Fig. 12–10). Work from the center out, not to shift wrinkles, but to keep the layers in place. Stitch a row, smooth the quilt and check for shifting, and sew the next row.

Machine Settings

To sew long, straight quilting rows, adjust pressure on the presser foot, experimenting to see what best suits your fabric, machine, and abilities. Try various machine feet like a roller foot or an embroidery foot (or spring). These will allow thick layers to pass under the needle more easily.

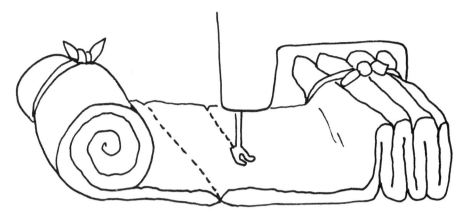

Fig. 12–10 To handle bulk while machine quilting, roll or accordion-fold the ends, then tie or safety pin. Make sure layers do not shift.

Make sure the bobbin is full, and that you have two or three extras wound with the right color thread. It's very frustrating to try to rewind and replace a bobbin with a quilt wedged into the machine. Make sure the quilt does not rub against the thread spool or cone, causing breakage. Clean the fuzzy lint out of your machine often as you sew. Make sure you have enough needles the right size and type on hand.

Using Hoops for Machine Sewing

Sewing machine hoops are made to fit under the presser foot, meaning they are not as thick as hand embroidery hoops. Even so, you may have to raise the presser foot that last fraction to get it under. The small 4″ to 8″ hoops have a spring on the top inner hoop for quick changes. It can be repositioned fairly easily as you move along. These are great for machine embroidery, but usually pop off thicker quilts. For quilts, use an adjustable hoop with a screw for enlarging it.

To use a hand embroidery hoop on a machine, put both sections of it under the needle by removing the presser foot (and possibly the needle), and sliding it under standing on edge. To move to a new area, leave the hoop under the presser foot and reposition it on the quilt. This will be a little difficult because the machine bed isn't a large flat area, but you may be able to manage. This is not ideal, but it may be the only way when you need a big hoop.

Choosing a Quilting Pattern

Quilting lines create organized texture in a quilt. Keep this in mind and relate your quilting pattern to the overall design. Choose machine quilting patterns that run in continuous straight or curved lines for easiest quilting. If the pattern makes circles or sharp turns, consider free-motion or hand quilting.

To stitch quilting lines, you have at least four alternatives:

1. Stitch-in-the-ditch is the least obtrusive way to quilt. Select major seam

lines, along the edges of blocks, for example, and sew exactly on the seam. Done well, this will not be visible; you'll have to look on the back to see what you did.

2. Quilt around design shapes, 1/8″ from the seam line. Use a matching or contrasting thread (Fig. 12–11). When puffy filler is used, this gives a trapunto or sculptured effect.

3. Stitch a geometric or other design evenly all over the quilt. The Trenton Quilt has a daisy design (see Fig. 12–2); quilted fabric usually has a diamond grid.

4. Use any stitch you like: a stab or running hand stitch; or various machine stitches, such as straight stitch, satin stitch, scallop stitch or blanket stitch.

Pin-and-Stitch

Unless yours is a crib-sized quilt, you'll be dealing with a mountain of bulk. This will take muscle, so dress for action. Don't wear shorts. The straight pins in quilts attack when least expected.

I'm assuming that your quilt is liberally safety-pin-basted or hand-basted

Fig. 12–11 A machine appliquéd block on the Birmingham quilt is outline quilted in contrasting white for decorative effect.

184

at 6″ to 12″ intervals, *not* on stitch lines. On the seam you plan to sew, place 2″ straight pins at right angles to the stitching line at 6″ intervals along the full length.

To begin, lower the presser foot, lower and raise the needle to pull the bobbin thread up, and hold the tails out of the way for the first few stitches. Spread the fingers of one hand to hold and guide the fabric, and take hold of the fabric behind the needle to maintain pressure for taut stitching. You can help move the quilt along, but don't pull hard or you'll jam the needle on the needle plate. Sew until you need new handholds, stop, reposition your hands, move the bulk of the quilt, and continue in this manner until the quilt line is completed.

When you stop to reposition, do it with the needle down to hold the stitch line in place. If your machine stops electronically with the needle up, make sure the quilt has not pulled off the stitch line or bent the needle, and that you begin again on the exact stitching line.

Each line may take from 15 minutes to a half hour. Count the number of stitch lines, multiply by the time factor, and you can estimate how long it will take to finish the quilt. Don't try a marathon session if you can help it. This is tiring and you may get careless in quality or sew through your finger.

About those pins. Take them out just before you come to them or, if your machine will do it, sew over them and then remove them. Don't leave them in past one seam length because they fall out or scratch you. If you find a pin sewn into a finished quilt, push the sharp end out and clip it off with wire cutters.

Free-Motion Quilting

If your quilting pattern has curved or complicated angles, you may choose to direct the movement of the quilt to avoid wrestling around a lot of turns. To do this, prepare your machine to darn or free-motion stitch by loosening the pressure on the presser foot (and lowering the feed dogs or setting the machine to 0 stitches per inch) so the quilt moves freely under the foot.

To sew, use both hands with fingers spread like a hoop to hold the fabric down firmly on the face plate (or the stitch won't form). Move slowly and evenly to make the size stitches you want in the direction you want. Experiment with machine speed to see what combination of speed and movement works best for nice, even stitches.

Check the back to see if you have missed stitches. If so, hold the fabric more firmly on the plate, slow down, or use a machine embroidery hoop. Use the kind with a screw to make the outer hoop larger, and wrap it with narrow fabric tape to prevent slippage so it won't pop off like a spring hoop. A hoop is a bother to move constantly, but this may be necessary for the best results, especially quilting around motifs.

Knot Quilting by Hand or Machine

Crazy quilts were most commonly knotted to avoid more complication on an already busy surface design. Knotting can be done by hand or machine and is the quickest way to quilt. Even so, it takes time and must be done carefully.

To machine knot, set your machine for bar tacking or sewing on a button. This means a zigzag stitch at 0 length and narrow width. Quilt "in the ditch," where stitching will be least visible.

Thread your machine with threads that match top and bottom for least visibility. Roll or accordian-fold the quilt (see Fig. 12–10) and start in the center at one side. Bar tack at each intersection and move to the next. If you clip the top and bobbin threads after each bar tack, you'll use less thread and run less risk of shifting layers. However, it is faster to do the whole row and clip later.

To hand knot, use a 24″ quilt hoop to keep the quilt taut. To make invisible knots, sew with matching thread and make tiny bar tacks on the top. For the traditional method, use a yarn needle and a harmonizing yarn color (red was popular on the dark quilts of the past). Insert the needle from the reverse side, come up through all layers and pull the yarn through. Reinsert the needle ⅛″ away and pull the yarn through to the back. Tie a double knot and clip threads to ¾″ long.

Hand Quilting

Begin with the thread- or pin-basted quilt sandwich, with finished or raw edges. Use a 24″ quilting hoop: the inner hoop goes under the quilt for positioning and the outer hoop goes over the top to pull it taut. Use the adjustment screw to make it looser or tighter as needed. Use small, sharp needles, but with a needle eye big enough for the thread. Use quilting thread (it twists less), or wax your thread as they did in the old days.

If your quilt fabrics are soft and the batting thin, you may be able to quilt with running stitches. Poke the needle in and out up to five stitches and pull it through. To get stitching closer together, use the quilter's poke method called *stabbing*. One hand pokes the needle in from the top and the other receives it on the bottom and stabs it back through to the top. (Until you develop good aim at this, you'll well understand why they call it "stabbing".) Use a single strand of thread in a matching or harmonizing color.

You may choose to quilt-in-the-ditch, especially if you are outlining blocks or lattice, or you don't want your less than perfect quilting stitches to show. I'm in this category. As one who goes for the visual effect, it's a pain to spend hours hand quilting. However, if the effect requires hand quilting, there I am stabbing away, hoping nobody is going to start counting stitches per inch.

Most quilters stitch ⅛″ inside the stitch line to outline blocks and design motifs, with visible quilting stitches. This will emphasize the shape of the motif and also cause it to puff. Since these stitches show, you'll have to take more care to make them neat, small and regular. That's probably why I like to machine quilt. Read any of Chilton's good quilt books for more explicit information on hand and machine quilting, but especially read Robbie and Tony Fanning's *Complete Book of Machine Quilting*.

Strip Quilting: Quilt-As-You-Go

This technique allows for much easier quilt wrestling—ahem, I mean manipulation. Single or double rows of blocks and lattice are assembled into the longest possible strips, either vertical or horizontal. At this point, the backing and bonded batting is cut into matching-size strips and pin- or hand-basted into long quilt sandwiches, one for each row or two of blocks.

These sandwich strips can then be quilted using one of the foregoing methods—free-motion machine quilting, presser-foot machine quilting, or hand quilting. The hoop will be easier to use for hand or machine quilting, with less bulk to handle (Fig. 12–12). For hand quilting, this technique is more portable.

As for edges, there are two ways to proceed:

1. You may choose to finish all edges on each strip, as described (the finish-before-you-finish method) and sew joining seams from the back. To do this, lay two strips face to face with edges matching, then hand-overcast or zigzag-machine stitch. Machine sew into both edges, with the left needle swing into the fabric and the right swing off.

2. For edges left unfinished, quilt to within 1 inch of the edges. Lay two

quilted block strips face to face, fold back the backing fabric on both sides, and hand or machine stitch the seam the full length, including only the quilt top and filler. To finish, lay one edge in place, fold a hem in the other and lay it in place. Hand or machine stitch. For more expert advice on this method of quilting, read Sandra Millet's *Quilt-As-You-Go.*

Quilting Frames

If you really get serious about quilting, it's worth getting a quilting frame. This device is usually made of long strips of wood the width of your quilt, plus additional pieces. The quilt is rolled on the front width beam and moved along to the back one as you quilt. This allows you to reach into the center of the quilt and keeps it taut for the whole quilting process.

Several people can work on a frame at once. Quilting bees allowed women to quilt together (usually during good travel weather) in the largest space available to set up their frames. They pieced blocks over the winter near the fire. Some evenings as I sit and sew, I can imagine the TV is a potbellied

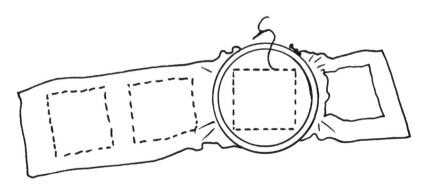

Fig. 12–12 Strip quilting by hand or machine allows working with smaller, less bulky units of the quilt.

stove, and I am making a keepsake for someone in the future to enjoy.

Binding the Edges

For quilts with unfinished edges, or for trimming finished edges, follow these steps:

1. Trim the edges of the quilt evenly, avoiding cutting hand sewn quilting stitches.

2. Cut binding strips on the diagonal, about 2″ wide or as desired. A 2″- wide binding folded lengthwise has ¼″ seam allowances and is ¾″ wide. Join bias strips with the grain to make an angled seam.

3. Fold the binding over the edges and hand sew. Or, to machine sew, unfold the binding, sew the binding to the quilt face, stitching on the seam allowance fold. Leave extra fabric at the corners. Fold the binding over and hand sew, or machine sew—making sure to catch the lower binding edge in the seam.

Colleen's Wedding Quilt

QUILT PROFILE

OCCASION: Quilt presented October 1, a week before the wedding of Colleen Cochran and Michael Nessle

QUILT DESIGNER: Lois Vosburg Goodrich

ORGANIZATION: Kits, including a background square and appliqué swatches, were mailed to friends and relatives of the bride and bridegroom. Returned squares were assembled and the quilt completed in time to be displayed with wedding gifts.

THEME: "They had interesting friends, so I suggested they each do something characteristic," Lois said.

TECHNIQUE: Appliqué fabric swatches and background square provided. Techniques included appliqué by hand and machine, and hand and machine embroidery.

TIME: Three months

SIZE: 81″ × 96″

BLOCK AND LAYOUT: Twenty 12″-square blocks, 4 across, 5 high; 3″ lattice; 3″ and 9″ borders, ½″ binding

COLORS: Off-white cotton background blocks; appliqué designs in tan and pink solids, rusty red, dark blue, and green pindots; rusty red pindot border; green pindot lattice; rusty red edging

FABRIC: Natural muslin, quilting cottons

YARDAGE TOTAL: 18⅓ yards 45″ fabric

FILLER: Bonded polyester quilt batt

QUILTING METHOD: Hand-quilted by professional Amish quilters, who charge by the yard of thread used.

DISPLAY: Wall hung

Chapter 13

Displaying Quilts

The Birmingham Bicentennial Quilt

At last your friendship quilt is completed. All the squares found homes on the quilt face, the lattice and border fabrics frame each block beautifully, the quilting stitches inpart a dimensional quality.

Next comes the presentation. Sometimes this event lacks drama: for example, I simply took Lori's to the post office and sent it to her in Denver. But I yearned to go along to see her face. With luck and good planning, you'll be able to join in a real "presentation." Giving Peter and Sandy their quilt was most satisfying. I finished hand-quilting the layers just before their Christmas wedding. We flew to Philadelphia with the quilt in a bag under my arm, and joined my sister and her family for the hurried car ride to the rehearsal dinner in Bethlehem, Pennsylvania. Peter paced outside the restaurant, worrying about everyone's safety on the snowy roads.

What fun for everyone to hug and kiss, and then present the quilt to Sandy and Peter. Everyone there— bridesmaids, moms, grandmothers, aunts, cousins, and friends—had made a square. The quilt was passed around in the candlelight for everyone to admire. Of course, all eyes darted first to

their own squares to see how they fit. The next day the bride's mother brought the quilt to the wedding, where more people got to enjoy it. Lois, Peter's mom, said it gave her a chance to get to know Peter's new relatives and form bonds better than any other way she could think of.

Try to present your quilt along with related festivities. If possible, plan a presentation, not only for your own enjoyment, but for everyone else's pleasure too.

Bob Marshall, owner of the Minister's Retirement Quilt, is a man noted for assembling words into meaningful phrases. He is still at a loss to describe how overwhelmed he was when he first saw his quilt.

Hanging a Quilt

Some people who receive quilts will display them on guest beds, but most will hang them on the wall. Hanging presents a problem, since almost nobody wants to put nail holes into a keepsake quilt.

Rod Pockets

If possible, make a rod pocket in the top of the quilt. It does not show when

Fig. 13–1 The Birmingham Bicentennial Quilt is a fine example of the group community quilts made around 1976. Rosemary Squires and friends made it as a gift to their town.

Fig. 13–2 Historical research unearthed photos of early town buildings and scenes, which contributors used on quilt blocks.

you use the quilt, and it makes hanging the quilt much easier. Ideally, you should incorporate the rod pocket while assembling the quilt, as described in Chapter 12.

To make a rod pocket on a completed quilt, follow these steps:

1. Select a ribbon or fabric strip for the rod pocket. Use matching blanket edging—a ribbon about 4″ wide that comes in packets, or use matching or coordinated fabric in a long strip the width necessary to accommodate the rod.

2. Determine what size rod you need to hold the quilt. To determine the right size, try various rods and drape the quilt over them to see if they sag in the center. A 1″-diameter extendable metal curtain rod may be fine, or you may need a stronger wooden rod. If a rod has large knobs on each end, make the slot large enough to accommodate the knob, unless the finial is removable or the rod comes apart in the middle to expand.

3. Determine the width of the rod pocket. Once you've chosen the right size rod, multiply the diameter of the rod by two for the width of the ribbon. A 1″ rod will measure 3.14″ around. (To determine this distance, multiply the diameter by 3.14, for the circumference.) This 1″ rod requires a 2″ ribbon, plus the 2″ of quilt backing, which equals a 4-inch diameter slot.

4. Measure the width of the quilt, and cut a piece of ribbon or fabric this length, plus 1″ for hems.

5. Turn and press narrow hems on each side, the length of the ribbon. Turn and press a rolled hem (two folds) at each end.

6. Hand or machine sew the hems at each end of the ribbon.

7. Align the ribbon with the top edge of the quilt on the back side. Fold back the ribbon so the reverse side of the ribbon abuts the top edge of the quilt. Hand or machine sew the ribbon along the hemmed edge to the quilt. Double stitch at each end to hold firmly.

8. Fold the ribbon down on the top edge of the quilt. You'll probably have to hand sew this last seam. If you are skilled with your machine, fold the hemmed edge and the quilt backing as for hemming a skirt, and stitch along this seam with a blind hem stitch.

Velcro Strips

Velcro strips are used to hang most exhibition quilts. Velcro consists of two fabric strips with tiny plastic loops on one strip, and tiny hooks on the other. Press them together and they will cling firmly until you pull them apart. Buy the necessary length to reach across the width of the quilt. For heavier quilts, buy wider Velcro. Hand or machine stitch one strip to the back of the quilt at the top edge, sewing around all the edges firmly. To store, stick the two strips together. To hang, staple or tack the other strip to the wall. Then stick the quilt's Velcro strip to the one on the wall.

Fig. 13–3 Jim Balmer made this early-model car, appropriate for Birmingham with many automotive business employees.

Bamboo Rods

For a lightweight quilt, you can use a bamboo rod. Make a rod pocket in the quilt or sew the bamboo rod to the quilt. Use double-weight sturdy thread and sew the rod in place, making long looping stitches over the rod.

Drapery Hooks

If you have a hanging rail or plan to hang the quilt on a drapery rod, use drapery hooks (with a pin end) on the top edge of the quilt. These may leave holes in the fabric, so drapery hooks are the last choice.

Displaying a Community Quilt

The Birmingham, Michigan, Bicentennial Quilt came together in 1976 under the stewardship of Rosemary Squires. It's not technically a friendship quilt (one made by a group of friends for another). Even so, a great many friends worked on it for the benefit of the community.

The quilt hangs on the wall at the Birmingham Community House behind sheets of Plexiglas for protection. The Plexiglas, in two large pieces, is mounted a few inches from the wall to allow air circulation over the fabric for preservation. A similar quilt in a nearby community—one of many Bicentennial quilts created around the country—has an enclosed case with small vents for air circulation.

Rosemary got us all involved in the Birmingham quilt. It has 42 squares depicting historic buildings or scenes; the committee, with advice from the

Fig. 13–4 An ice pond scene, appliquéd and embroidered for the Birmingham Bicentennial Quilt.

quilt, it was stretched on a quilting frame and patient quilters outlined every shape or figure within the squares and around the quilt blocks.

A quilt like this, enormous in size and complex in detail, has impressive monetary value by completion. Other communities who did Bicentennial quilts debated the cost of having a huge display case made. When they found that their quilts appraised in the thousands of dollars, spending a couple of hundred for the display did not seem too costly.

Displaying the Birmingham Church Quilt

People are always looking for good ideas for fund raisers. Raffling off a

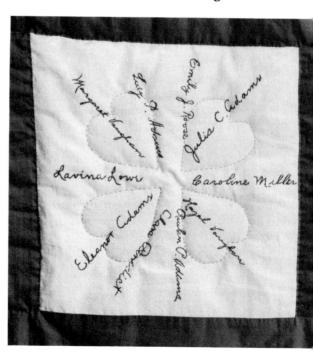

Fig. 13–5 In 1902, church members and friends bought places for their signatures on the Birmingham Presbyterian Church quilt.

Historical Commission, sorted through photos, slides and on-site drawings to choose the scenes.

This quilt follows the pattern of group quilts. It was designed and created by a large group of people; six workshops were held at the Birmingham Bloomfield Art Association so people could choose their scenes and sort through a huge mound of coordinated fabrics, all washed and ironed, ready for use. Everyone enjoyed the sewing bee atmosphere surrounding these get-togethers. People taking classes in the various studios, visitors to the gallery, and staff all wandered through during the quilting to check on progress. After assembling the

194

friendship or group quilt can be a successful money maker. The Birmingham Presbyterian Church Quilt, made in 1902, raffled off squares. Parishioners bought the squares, and then sold space to their friends for their signatures. A square with 12 names could bring in $12, and 20 squares could bring in $240. This may sound like a small sum now, but it was considerable in 1902. The quilt now hangs in the church conference room.

Displaying the quilt in a central location helps sell raffle tickets. Each person can imagine that beautiful quilt on his own bed, keeping him cozy and warm. One lady was so thrilled to be the winner of a raffled quilt that she

Fig. 13–6 The Birmingham Presbyterian Church Quilt, laid away unquilted for years, now hangs completed in a conference room at the church, available to geneaology searchers for study.

invited 60 friends to a viewing party to admire it.

A group of California quilters chooses a theme, and each member embroiders a square for the quilt so exquisite that anyone would buy a fistful of chances. If you have an energetic group of quilters who need to raise money, this is a good way to do it.

Caring for Your Quilt

Washability

The Birmingham Bicentennial Quilt could tolerate washing, with its preshrunk fabric and hand sewing, but many friendship quilts with glued-on parts or crayon drawings would be difficult to wash. In the days of hand washing, a wet quilt was too heavy to cope with, so householders avoided washing it altogether if they could manage. Generally, friendship quilts were and are meant as keepsake quilts, to be saved and treasured—and rarely washed.

If you must wash a friendship quilt, use a gentle soap such as Woolite for wools, synthetics, and "unknown" fibers; use Cotton Wash for all-cotton, linen, or other natural fibers. Soak in cool water, don't scrub or rub vigorously. Spin the quilt in the washing

Fig. 13–7 Claudia's Wedding Quilt is displayed on Grandfather Hall's carved wooden bed now in her possession.

machine to remove excess water, and smooth it out to dry. Hanging a wet quilt may pull it out of shape, so hang it over several parallel clothes lines, or clothes racks, or lay it flat to dry. Shift it now and then to dry all areas. Do not dry it in direct sun.

Dry cleaning may work for a soiled quilt, unless it has painted squares, trim such as sequins that may disintegrate, crayon transfer drawings, glue-on pieces, or plastic, fur or leather parts.

Surface Protection

The best care for a quilt is to display it out of direct sunlight. Brush it weekly with a hand brush or vacuum cleaner wand to remove settling dust. Give it a fluffing now and then. You can spray a quilt with ScotchGuard if you live in an area with a lot of airborne dirt. Test a small area of the quilt to see if the spray causes any problems, such as bleeding color.

Storage

When you put your quilt away, roll it, or fold it slightly differently each time to avoid permanent creases.

Experts say you should *not* store your quilt sealed in a plastic bag, since the fibers need to breathe or they'll deteriorate.

Repairs

If some of the fabrics on your quilt begin to deteriorate, as fragile silks will after many years, buy the sheerest, best quality fabric available, and cover worn squares. The original fabric and details will show through, yet will be held in place by the fabric covering.

For loose stitches, thread your needle with matching thread and carefully repair seams, appliqués, or embroideries. With some practice you can develop a skilled hand, and no one can tell what you repaired. Antique experts may insist that you devalue a quilt by repair, but if it's your own friendship quilt and you don't plan to sell it, keep it in the best shape possible for future generations.

I can just hear my granddaughter, Hattie Stroud, in 2010 when she is about to be married, quizzing her mother about Claudia's Wedding Quilt made back in 1981. "Who made this one, Mom?" Claudia may say, "Oh, I haven't thought of that friend for ages. . ." and she'll smile with the memories.

CHART FOR RECORDING YOUR QUILTS

OWNER OR NAME OF QUILT: _____

OCCASION: _____

PARTICIPANTS: _____

_____

QUILT DESIGNER: _____

ORGANIZATION METHOD: _____

THEME: _____

TECHNIQUE: _____

DATE/TIME TO MAKE: _____

QUILT SIZE: _____

BLOCK NUMBER AND SIZE: _____

LAYOUT: _____

COLORS: _____

_____

FABRICS: _____

_____

YARDAGE TOTALS: _____

_____

FILLER: _____

QUILTING METHOD: _____

DISPLAY: _____

SUPPLIES AND CONSTRUCTION: _____

_____

Sources of Supply

Threads
Aardvark Adventures, PO Box 2449, Livermore, CA 94550

Art Sales, 4801 W. Jefferson, Los Angeles, CA 90016

D&E Distributing, 199 El Camino Real, #F-242, Encinitas, CA 92024

J&P Coats and Clark, PO Box 6044, Norwalk, CT 06852

Speed Stitch Inc., PO Box 3472, Port Charlotte, FL 33949

Swiss-Metrosene Inc., 7780 Quincy St., Willowbrook, IL 60521

White Sewing Machine Co., 11750 Berea Rd., Cleveland, OH 44111

Fabrics
Cabin Fever Fabrics, PO Box 54, Center Sandwich, NH 03227 (catalogue, $2.75)

Patchwork Crafts, PO Box 1171-Q-9, Taylor, SC 29687

Stretch & Sew Fabrics Swatch Club, 7100 Brookfield Plaza, Springfield, VA 22150

Filler
Buffalo Batt & Felt Corp., Dept. T-10, 3307 Walden Ave., Depew, NY 14043

Fairfield Processing Corp., PO Box 1130, Danbury, CT 06810

Hobbs Bonded Fibers, Craft Products Division, PO Box 151, Goresbeck, TX 76642

Sewing Supplies
Sew-Art International, PO Box 550, 412 South 425 West, Bountiful, UT 84010 (water-soluble machine embroidery facing, etc., catalogue, $2)

Sewing Emporium, 1087 Third Ave., Chula Vista, CA 92010

Copiers and Enlargers
Foster Trent, Inc., Dept. 410-K, 2345 Boston Post Road, Larchmont, NY 10538

Norton Products, Dept. GT-45, Box 2012, New Rochelle, NY 10802

Miscellaneous
Binney & Smith Inc., Easton, PA 18044-0431 (transfer crayons)

C-Thru Ruler Co., 6 Britton Drive, Box 356, Bloomfield, CT 06002 (rulers, templates)

Suggested Reading

Better Homes and Gardens' Creative Machine Stitchery. New York: Meredith, 1985.

Better Homes and Gardens, editors. *The Pleasures of Counted Cross-stitch*. New York: Meredith, 1984.

Devlin, Nancy. *Guide to Machine Quilting*. Starshine Stitchery Press (privately published).

Fairfield, Helen. *Patchwork*. London: Octopus Books, 1984.

Fanning, Robbie and Tony. *The Complete Book of Machine Quilting*. Radnor, PA: Chilton, 1980.

Frager, Dorothy. *The Quilting Primer*, second ed., Radnor, PA: Chilton, 1979.

Guild, Vera P. *The Creative Use of Stitches*. Worcester, MA: Davis Publications, 1964, 1969.

Hall, Carolyn Vosburg. *A to Z Soft Animals*. New York: Prentice-Hall, 1986.

———. *The Sewing Machine Crafts Book*. New York: Van Nostrand Reinhold, 1980 (now distributed by Prentice-Hall).

———. *Soft Sculpture*. Worcester, MA: Davis Publications, 1981.

———. *Stitched and Stuffed Art*. New York: Doubleday, 1974.

Hall, Carrie A., and Rose Kretsinger. *The Romance of the Patchwork Quilt*. New York: Crown Publishers, Bonanza imprint, 1935.

Holstein, Jonathan. *The Pieced Quilt*. New York Graphic Society, 1973.

Hopkins, Mary Ellen. *The It's Okay if You Sit on My Quilt Book*. Westminster, CA: Burdette Publications, 1982.

Leone, Diane. *The Sampler Quilt*. Santa Clara, CA: Leone Press, 1985.

Lipsett, Linda Otto. *Remember Me*. New York: The Quilt Digest Press, 1985.

McKim, Ruby. *101 Patchwork Patterns*. Dover, DE: Dover Press, 1962.

Index